GANDHI
GREAT SOUL

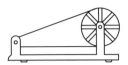

GANDHI
GREAT SOUL

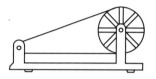

BY JOHN B. SEVERANCE

CLARION BOOKS

NEW YORK

FRONTISPIECE: Wood engraving by American artist Fritz Eichenberg, from the Special Collection of the University of Rhode Island. © 1997 Fritz Eichenberg Trust/Licensed by VAGA, New York, N.Y.

Clarion Books
a Houghton Mifflin Company imprint
215 Park Avenue South, New York, NY 10003
Text copyright © 1997 by John B. Severance.

For information about this and other Houghton Mifflin trade and reference books and multimedia products, visit The Bookstore at Houghton Mifflin on the World Wide Web at (http://www.hmco.com/trade/).

Book design by Sylvia Frezzolini Severance.
Type is 12.5 point Sabon.
Printed in the USA

Library of Congress Cataloging-in Publication Data

Severance, John B.
    Gandhi, great soul / by John B. Severance.
        p.   cm.
    Includes bibliographical references and index.
    ISBN 0-395-77179-X
    1. Gandhi, Mahatma, 1869–1947—Juvenile literature.
   2. Nationalists—India—Biography—Juvenile literature.   I. Title.
DS481.G3S465   1997
954.03'5'092—dc20   95-20887
                                                             CIP
                                                             AC

KPT   10   9   8   7   6   5   4   3   2   1

For my daughters
Rebecca and Abigail.
Each, in her own way,
is a seeker of truth
and love.

CONTENTS

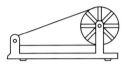

*Mohandas K. Gandhi as a Satyagrahi in
South Africa about 1907.*

CHAPTER ONE

THE MESSAGE

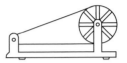

The great mission of Gandhi's life was to help the 350,000,000 people of India free themselves from British rule. "No people exists," he once wrote, "that would not think itself happier under its own bad government than it might really be under the good government of an alien power." Many peoples have struggled for independence. They have resorted to terrorism and fought bloody battles. Gandhi's revolution was different from others in history. He believed that people could free themselves from tyranny without using violent tactics.

As a timid little boy, Mohandas Gandhi did not seem likely to become a great leader. Later, as an elegantly dressed young law student in London, he seemed particularly interested in becoming thoroughly English. In his twenty years of asserting the rights of Indian immigrants in South Africa he was not in rebellion against the British Empire. At the outbreak of the First World War, Gandhi even helped recruit Indians to fight for England. During all this time, however, he was growing spiritually. Mohandas was developing a way of life that would eventually earn him the name *Mahatma*. In Sanskrit, the ancient language of India, the word means "Great Soul."

Gandhi was also a gifted politician. In the Western world, religion and politics are usually separate. In the United States, the doctrine of "separation of Church and State" began with the founding of the country. In India, it is difficult to separate the two. For the Hindu Gandhi, it was impossible. Hindu ways and beliefs govern daily life and cannot be separated from everyday politics. The Hindu way became Gandhi's line of communication with millions of Indian peasants. It was the only means he could find to teach them to respect themselves and resist British domination. Gandhi thought the people had to have self-respect to believe in their own human rights. They would then have the mental strength to seek a nonviolent route to *swaraj*, or self-rule.

During the years of struggle for independence, a quarter of the Indian population was Muslim. Gandhi believed that Muslims and Hindus had to cooperate if the movement for swaraj was to succeed. Most of the time Hindus and Muslims got along together in peace, but not always. Moments of bitter hatred sometimes exploded in terrible violence and bloodshed. Gandhi pointed out that strife between Hindus and Muslims gave the British a powerful excuse to continue their rule in India.

Another group of people Gandhi insisted on including in the struggle was the "untouchables." These people were mostly Hindu. They were the very lowest in the class structure of Hindu society.

The highest class, or caste, the Brahmins, considered themselves unclean if they ever touched members of the lowest group. The untouchables were casteless or outcaste. They were allowed employment in only the most undesirable jobs such as sweeping the streets or cleaning latrines. Some of them tried to change their rank by becoming Christians or Muslims. The majority of them lived in filth and humiliation. Gandhi said this was obviously a gross injustice built into the Hindu way. Swaraj could only be honestly achieved if the rest of India learned to live with and love the untouchables. Otherwise, self-rule would be exchanging one tyranny for another.

Gandhi believed that all people in the world are brothers and sisters. He did not hate the English. In fact, he saw a lot that was good about them. It was to that good that he wanted to appeal for swaraj. He thought that patient, peaceful resistance to an oppressive government would eventually persuade the British Empire to see for itself the dishonesty and injustice of its colonial system. Gandhi called this nonviolent means of revolution *satyagraha,* which is a combination of two Sanskrit words, *satya,* meaning truth and love, plus *agraha,* meaning firmness.

Satyagraha sent waves around the world. In 1951, a young black South African named Nelson Mandela described the concept to a crowd in Johannesburg. "Volunteering was a difficult and even dangerous duty," he explained in his autobiography, "as the authorities would seek to intimidate, imprison, and perhaps attack the volunteers. . . . No matter what the authorities did, the volunteers could not retaliate. . . . They must respond to violence with nonviolence." Later on, Mandela modified his views on nonviolence. "For me nonviolence was not a moral principle but a strategy." If

President of South Africa Nelson Mandela.

American civil rights leader, Dr. Martin Luther King, Jr.

nonviolence did not work he would try something else. Nevertheless, Mandela was attracted to the idea of satyagraha and said of Gandhi, "I have always found him a great source of inspiration."

At about the same time Mandela was explaining nonviolent resistance in Johannesburg, Dr. Mordecai W. Johnson, president of Howard University in Washington, D.C., gave a lecture in Philadelphia about Mahatma Gandhi. In the audience was a young theological student named Martin Luther King, Jr. He was so taken with the idea of satyagraha that he went out and bought half a dozen books on the Mahatma. Only a few years after the Philadelphia lecture, King, who had often hated whites, stood in front of a crowd in Montgomery, Alabama. "Hate begets hate," he said. "Violence begets violence. . . . We must meet the forces of hate with soul force. Our aim must never be to defeat or humiliate the white man, but to win his friendship and understanding." In 1959, he and his wife, Coretta Scott King, took a trip to India to meet some of the people who had known Gandhi. For Dr. Martin Luther King, Jr., satyagraha was a moral principle.

Satyagraha is Gandhi's message to the world and the centuries to come.

Top: *Gandhi's parents, Karamchand and Putliba.*
Bottom: *Mohandas K. Gandhi at age 7.*

CHAPTER TWO

YOUNG MOHANDAS

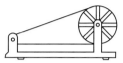

Victoria, Queen of Great Britain and Ireland, was exactly halfway through her sixty-four-year reign when Mohandas Karamchand Gandhi was born on October 2, 1869, in Porbandar on the shore of the Arabian Sea. When Mohandas was eight years old, the words *Empress of India* were added to the queen's titles. The British Empire was reaching the peak of its strength and glory. Most Englishmen took it for granted that the empire, which included vast territories on all the continents, was the most civilized government the world had ever known. A great many other people in distant parts of the empire took comfort in British protection.

The British had gained full political control of the Indian subcontinent only twelve years before Gandhi was born. They had been establishing their power gradually since 1803. For the three centuries before that, most of India had been dominated by the

*Victoria, Queen of
Great Britain and Ireland,
and Empress of India.*

Mogul Empire, which was built by Muslim invaders from Turkey and Afghanistan. This once-mighty empire became weak and broken due to civil wars. By the time the British arrived, most of India was a collection of Muslim-ruled principalities governing millions of Hindus. The population of India also included Buddhists, Zoroastrians, Jews, Christians, and many Muslims, but the vast majority of people were Hindu.

Mohandas was born into a prominent Hindu family of the Vaisya caste. This was the third-ranking caste in the class structure of Hinduism. The first was the Brahmin, the caste of priests and teachers. The second was the Kshatriya caste for princes and warriors. The third, Gandhi's, was for farmers and merchants. The fourth caste was the Sudra, who were craftsmen and peasants. Millions of Hindus, the lowly untouchables, belonged to no caste at all. Within each caste there were many subcastes. The whole system was so complex that in Gandhi's lifetime it had begun to disintegrate. Gandhi's father and grandfather were not farmers or merchants. In fact, they were prime ministers of the tiny principality of Porbandar on the Kathiawar Peninsula in the state of Gujarat.

Today, visitors may see Gandhi's first home in Porbandar.

To Mohandas, the spiritual side of Hinduism was much more important than the caste system. His spirituality began with his mother's extremely religious nature and continued to dominate his thoughts and actions for the rest of his life. Hinduism is such an ancient way of life that no one knows who its founder was or even if there was one. Because Hinduism absorbed many religions and sects in its five thousand years of growth, it has taken many forms in various parts of India. One of its most sacred texts is the Bhagavad Gita, or "Song of the Lord." It is a long poem, a discussion between the god Krishna and a prince named Arjuna, before a battle in a civil war. In the course of the discussion, Krishna explains that in life the struggle for peace must be fought "free from the sense of 'I' and 'mine.' " As a boy, Mohandas often heard portions of the Gita read aloud, but he did not actually read it himself until he was a law student in London. For the rest of his life he regarded it as his spiritual guide.

Mohandas's spiritual education actually began long before he read the Gita. His mother, Putliba Gandhi, said prayers before each meal and visited the nearby temple every day. Sometimes she fasted, went without food, as part of her religious devotion. She would make some sort of fast during the four-month rainy season known as *Chaturmas*, a period rather like the Christian Lent. One season she fasted every other day. During another Chaturmas she decided to eat only when the sun came out. "We children," Gandhi wrote in his autobiography, "would stand, staring at the sky, waiting to announce the appearance of the sun to our mother." Whenever it suddenly came out, Mohandas, his two brothers, and his sister would all rush into the house to tell her she could eat. "She would

Mohandas on the right at age 14, with his older brother Laxmidas.

run to see with her own eyes but by that time the fugitive sun would be gone, thus depriving her of her meal. 'That does not matter,' she would say cheerfully. 'God did not want me to eat today.' And then she would return to her round of duties."

Also in his autobiography Gandhi reported that his early school days were not outstanding. "It was with some difficulty that I got through my multiplication tables. The fact that I recollect nothing more of those days than having learnt, in company with other boys, to call our teacher all kinds of names, would strongly suggest that my intellect must have been sluggish." Although he joined his classmates in making fun of their teacher, Mohandas had only a few friends. He was smaller and skinnier than most boys his age and his ears stuck out. He was afraid other children might make fun of him, so he usually ran home after school to look after his houseplants or do homework. At home he sometimes got into mischief, but no one could resist his charming smile.

In 1879 the Gandhi family moved to Rajkot, an inland town in Gujarat, because Gandhi's father, Karamchand, had been appointed prime minister of the princely state of Rajkot. Mohandas attended a grade school for two years, and at the age of twelve entered Alfred Boys High School. More than a century later, the school continues. The chiseled stone letters over the entrance still say "Alfred High School," although the official name is now Mahatma Gandhi High School in honor of its most famous alumnus.

A bell to ring the changing of classes still hangs in the main corridor of Alfred High School.

Students still attend Alfred High School, now renamed Mahatma Gandhi High School in honor of its most famous graduate.

When he was thirteen Mohandas was married to a thirteen-year-old Porbandar girl named Kasturba. Such marriages were not at all unusual during Gandhi's childhood. They were arranged by the families, and the two getting married were not consulted. The engagements often took place years in advance, when the children were much too young to know what was happening. The whole Gandhi family went to Porbandar for the wedding, which, like

A festive Hindu wedding similar to the one celebrated by Mohandas and Kasturba.

most Hindu weddings, was elaborate and festive. Kasturba was the daughter of a prosperous merchant who lived only a few houses away from the Gandhi house in Porbandar. Even though her upbringing was well-to-do, Kasturba was illiterate and remained so for the sixty-two years of the marriage. The young couple did not have to worry about setting up a household. It was the custom for newlyweds to live with the bridegroom's family for a few years. The bride was allowed to go live with her parents every few months.

For a teenage boy whose schoolwork was mediocre, marriage was a serious distraction. Gandhi was a domineering husband who insisted his wife ask his permission whenever she wanted to leave the house. When Mohandas was sixteen, his father became extremely ill. The son was conscientious about nursing Karamchand, but one night he decided he needed a break. He turned the job over to his uncle and went to get into bed with Kasturba. Quite suddenly, Karamchand died. Some weeks later, Kasturba's first baby died soon after it was born. Mohandas believed the sad event was his punishment for having sex with his wife at the moment his father passed away. Before they turned eighteen the young couple became the parents of their first surviving son, Harilal.

Mohandas continued his education but was unsettled about his direction in life. After discussing the future with an old family friend, a Brahmin priest, it was decided that Gandhi should go to England to study law. With a law degree he might be able to inherit his father's old position as prime minister of Porbandar.

Arrangements for the journey involved many negotiations with family, friends, and government officials. Money was not the only problem. His mother was opposed to the project. To appease her, he had to swear never to touch alcohol, women, or meat. The vow could not have been difficult as Gujaratis do not drink alcohol and are strict vegetarians. Furthermore, Mohandas would not have wanted to be unfaithful to Kasturba. In August 1888, Gandhi said good-bye to Kasturba and traveled to Bombay to take a steamer to London. In Bombay, a council of members of his caste informed him that travel abroad would ruin his standing as a Hindu. He was forbidden to go to England. Mohandas informed them politely that it was not their business and that he intended to make the voyage. Long after he boarded the ship, their condemnation must have been ringing in his ears. "This boy shall be treated as an outcaste from today," said the head of the council and announced that anyone who went to see him off at the docks would be fined.

During the three-week voyage, Mohandas spent most of his time in his cabin. He thought his English was not yet good enough for conversation with the other passengers. The dining room presented an additional problem. "I was innocent of the use of knives and forks," Gandhi wrote later, "and had not the boldness to inquire what dishes on the menu were free of meat. I therefore never took meals at table but always had them in my cabin, and they consisted principally of sweets and fruit which I had brought with me." He wore his dark suits throughout the voyage to save his white summer flannel one for a smart appearance on arrival in England. As it was a cool and foggy day in late September when the boat docked in Southampton, he looked and felt very much out of place in the white suit. Two fellow passengers took Mohandas to one of the most elegant hotels in London. The bright lights and the fancy uniforms of the bellhops amazed him. He was even more astonished when what he thought was a small waiting room rose up and delivered him to another floor of the hotel. The young Indian had never seen an elevator.

Even after he found a cheaper room, Mohandas continued to live a timid and uncomfortable life in London until he decided to become an English gentleman. He spent money he could not afford on expensively tailored suits with the elegant accessories of top hat, leather gloves, and a silver-headed walking stick. He also made arrangements for a variety of lessons, including dancing and violin. "But it was beyond me to achieve anything like rhythmic motion," wrote Gandhi. "And how could dancing make a gentleman of me? The violin I could learn even in India. I was a student and should get on with my studies. . . . If my character made a gentleman of me, so much the better."

The student did get on with his studies. He also discovered vegetarian restaurants, joined the London Vegetarian Society, and made new friends, One of these, Sir Edwin Arnold, had translated the Bhagavad Gita from Sanskrit into English. Mohandas read the translation and was deeply impressed. Another friend gave him a Bible. He didn't gain much from the Old Testament, but in the New

The London Vegetarian Society, 1890. Gandhi is lower right.

London-trained lawyer, Mohandas K. Gandhi, about 1890.

Testament he discovered Christ's Sermon on the Mount, which he said went straight to his heart. "The verses, 'But I say unto you, that ye resist not evil: but whosoever shall smite thee on thy right cheek, turn to him the other also. And if any man take away thy coat let him have thy cloke too,' delighted me beyond measure." The Sermon reminded Gandhi of certain passages in the Gita. At this time the young law student also read books on Buddha and Mohammed. As a result, some aspects of Christian, Buddhist, and Muslim thinking entered his Hindu philosophy of life. By the time he passed his bar examination Gandhi's education included a great deal more than the knowledge of the law for which he had traveled so far.

In the summer of 1891, Mohandas returned to India. His older brother, Laxmidas, met him at the dock in Bombay and told him that their mother had died, a few weeks earlier. Gandhi felt even greater grief than when his father died but there was no time to show it. The family expected a great deal of him and he had a career to seek. After his London experience, Rajkot seemed like a backwater of civilization. He moved to Bombay to start a law practice. Finding himself tongue-tied at his first trial, he returned his client's money and moved back to Rajkot.

It was at this time that Gandhi had his first run-in with British authority. In London he had met a man named Charles Ollivant who was now the political officer in Rajkot. Laxmidas was having some political difficulties and asked his brother to put in a good word with Ollivant. Mohandas did not feel right about this but could not refuse his brother. He went to see Ollivant and was thrown out of the office. Gandhi knew he should not have tried to use his personal connection for a political purpose. Nevertheless, he felt he had been treated too harshly. He asked a prominent Indian lawyer from Bombay what legal action he might take. The reply came that Gandhi did not know how to get along with British *sahibs*. He should "pocket the insult" if he expected to make a living as a lawyer in Rajkot. Stunned, Gandhi vowed that never again would he put himself in such an awkward position. Later, in his autobiography, he wrote, "This shock changed the course of my life." The birth of his second son, Manilal, in October of 1892, was the only bright spot in a dismal time for Mohandas. He was lost in his own country.

A partner in the Porbandar office of the ship-owning and trading business Dada Abdulla and Company offered Mohandas a chance to escape his frustrations. The merchant was involved in a complicated lawsuit against a relative in Johannesburg, Transvaal, South Africa. The lawyers already on the case were European and there was need for advice from an Indian lawyer. Gandhi was offered a year's work at the company's South African office in the port of Durban. He jumped at the opportunity.

Not long after his arrival in Durban, Gandhi was sent to attend the trial, which was taking place in Pretoria, the capital of the Republic of Transvaal. The Transvaal had been settled by Boer farmers of Dutch descent. Durban was in the British Crown Colony of Natal. There was no direct train line from Durban to Pretoria. The train ran from Durban to Charlestown, which was near the border of the Transvaal. Then there was a long stagecoach ride to Johannesburg and then another train to Pretoria. Gandhi was given a first-class ticket for the four-day trip. The first train made a stop at 9 P.M. at Pietermaritzburg, capital of Natal. While the train was in the station, a railroad official ordered him to ride in the baggage car. Gandhi replied that he had a first-class ticket and intended to remain in the first-class compartment. A police officer was called in to remove Gandhi from the train. He was taken to the waiting room and his baggage was locked up.

Mohandas shivered all night in the cold winter air while his overcoat remained locked in the baggage room. He began to ponder his options. Should he give up and return to Durban and then to India? No. He was at least obligated to finish the company's business in Pretoria. What then? Go back to India and forget the nasty incident? What about the sixty-six thousand Indians, mostly poor laborers, in South Africa? Gandhi knew they all suffered the same discrimination he was just then experiencing. "The hardship to which I was subjected was superficial," he wrote in his autobiography, "only a symptom of the deep disease of colour prejudice. I should try, if possible, to root out the disease and suffer hardships in the process."

In Rajkot, Gandhi had received a shock that would change his life. Among the night shadows of a chilly South African railway station, he reached a decision that would change the lives of the thousands of Indians in South Africa, and the millions of people in India.

Gandhi when he was a prosperous lawyer in Johannesburg.

THE LONG APPRENTICESHIP

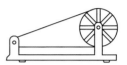

The rest of Gandhi's trip to Pretoria continued to be an experience in racial prejudice. The agent in charge of the stage-coach to Johannesburg would not allow Mohandas to ride in the coach with the other passengers. He was forced to ride outside next to the driver while the agent rode inside. At a stop along the way the agent tried to make him give up his seat and ride on the footboard of the driver's seat. "The insult was more than I could bear," wrote Gandhi in his autobiography. "In fear and trembling I said to him, 'Now that you want to sit outside and smoke, you would have me sit at your feet. I will not do so, but I am prepared to sit inside.' "

The agent punched Gandhi in the head and tried to drag him off the seat, but the determined young Indian hung on to a railing. The other passengers insisted that he be allowed to sit with them and the struggle was stopped. "My heart was beating fast," wrote

Gandhi, "and I was wondering if I should ever reach my destination alive." On the last leg of the journey, the train to Pretoria, an Englishman defended Gandhi's right to sit in a first-class compartment. The train conductor who had tried to make Gandhi move said to the Englishman, "If you want to travel with a coolie, what do I care?" *Coolie* was a name derived from the Hindi word for untouchable. Prejudiced South African whites used it as a demeaning and offensive nickname for anyone of Indian descent.

Indians began to arrive in South Africa in 1860 when English sugar growers in the coastal area of Natal needed a source of cheap labor. Since the native blacks already had simple and traditional means of supporting themselves, they did not want the harsh work of the plantations. The planters arranged for indentured laborers to come from across the Indian Ocean. These workers, mostly untouchables, were contracted for five years. They were given free room and board for their families and ten shillings (roughly five dollars) a month. At the end of five years of indenture laborers had a choice. Their fares back to India would be paid or they could remain in South Africa as freelance laborers. Many chose to stay. These people were hard workers and extremely thrifty. They became truck farmers and shopkeepers. The community was expanded by the arrival of Muslim and Hindu businessmen and professionals, merchants, doctors, and lawyers. In economic strength, Indians began to rival the dominant white community. By the time Gandhi arrived in South Africa there were approximately forty-three thousand Indians in Natal and forty thousand whites. Both groups were small minorities compared with the four hundred thousand native Zulus.

When Mohandas finished his business for Dada Abdulla, the all-white Natal legislature was about to pass a law that would deprive Indians of their right to vote. The proposed Franchise Amendment Bill claimed that no Indian could understand representative government because "he is a political infant of the most backward type." When Gandhi asked other Indians what they thought of the proposal, they shrugged and said there was no use fighting the white man. Gandhi took a different view. Indians were subjects of Queen Victoria and therefore entitled to the same rights as other citizens of the British Empire. If Indians did not insist on equal rights under the law, they would be agreeing that they were inferior to whites. They would lose their dignity as human beings. The young lawyer even took the argument one step further. If white people were allowed to assume they were superior to people of other colors, they too lost dignity as human beings. "It has always been a mystery to me," wrote Gandhi, "how men can feel themselves honored by the humiliation of their fellow beings."

Some wealthy Muslim Indian merchants asked Gandhi to postpone his planned return to India and his family. He agreed to stay one more month to help organize opposition to the Franchise Amendment Bill. A meeting of Indians was called that included some Christian youth groups of Natal-born Indians who became volunteers in the campaign. Muslims, Christians, and Hindus "were all agreeably surprised to find themselves taking a share in public work," wrote Gandhi. "All were alike the children and servants of the motherland." Under his direction, they sent telegrams to the Legislative Assembly and to the attorney general of Natal. The greatest effort was a petition sent to London with ten thousand

Indian signatures and addressed to the secretary of state for the colonies. This massive effort merely delayed the passage of the law.

The Franchise Amendment Bill was only one example of injustice to Indians living in South Africa. In Natal, Indians had to carry special passes after 9 P.M. In the Boer republics of the Orange Free State and the Transvaal, Indians were not allowed to own property and farm. In both British and Boer parts of South Africa, Indians could not own or buy land, and some local laws even forbade them to walk on public footpaths.

Gandhi's Indian friends now urged him to stay on in Natal indefinitely to help them fight for their rights. He agreed on the condition that he could earn his living. He set up a new law office in Durban but refused to charge legal fees for public work. Dada Abdulla gave him a house and furniture, and about twenty merchants agreed to send him their private legal work. This arrangement showed Gandhi's philosophical principles. He thought his income should not depend on charity. If he earned his living from private or commercial work, he could be more open with the merchants. "As your friend and servant," he told them, "I should occasionally have to say hard things to you. Heaven only knows whether I should retain your affection."

During the next three years Gandhi's law practice flourished. So did his career as a political leader and organizer. To keep the work going he founded the Natal Indian Congress. He wrote pamphlets and letters to be distributed not only in South Africa but in England and India as well. These appeals always centered on one point: Laws had to uphold the equality of all citizens of the British Empire. In a letter to the *Times of India,* Gandhi observed that it

The founders of the Natal Indian Congress. Gandhi is in the middle of the back row.

was not possible to prevent racial prejudice by making it illegal, but an unjust law was wrong in "feeding the prejudice by legalizing it."

By 1896 Gandhi realized that his work would keep him in South Africa for many years to come. He took six months leave to go home and bring Kasturba and their two sons to Natal. While he was in India, Gandhi wrote pamphlets and gave speeches proclaiming the unjust treatment of Indians living in South Africa. At this time he met several political leaders, including Gopal Krishna Gokhale, who became his political mentor. Much later Gandhi wrote, "In the sphere of politics the place that Gokhale occupied in my heart . . . was and is absolutely unique."

When several hundred Indian passengers plus Gandhi, two

sons, and Kasturba, pregnant with a third child, arrived on a steamer in Durban, South Africa, the Natal government would not allow them to land. While the ship was anchored outside the harbor for three weeks, the captain asked Gandhi how he felt about the authorities who were trying to stop him from returning to Natal. "I have no anger against them," he said. "I am only sorry for their ignorance and narrowness. I know that they sincerely believe that what they are doing today is right and proper." When he was finally permitted to go ashore, he was beaten up by a mob of whites. He was rescued by the wife of the police superintendent, who managed to protect him from the crowd until some policemen arrived on the scene. The news of the attack upset many people in England. Secretary of State for the Colonies Joseph Chamberlain sent word from London that the attackers should be prosecuted. Gandhi refused, saying it was not their fault but the fault of the Natal government. Under pressure from Chamberlain and from the British government in India, the Natal legislature passed a law establishing equal voting rights for all British subjects. This had been Gandhi's goal all along.

At this time in his life Gandhi was developing a philosophy of self-reliance. He felt that the concept could help the self-esteem of Indians. This in turn would help them resist injustice. Gandhi intended to set the example. His household, which included most of his legal staff, became a community of self-help. Gandhi learned to wash and iron his own clothes. He read medical books and became the house doctor. He even assisted at the birth of his third son, Ramdas, in 1897. Kasturba, the children, the law office clerks, and secretaries who lived in the house were all expected to share in the household tasks. There was no running water in the house and therefore no toilets. One of the tasks was to take the chamber pots outside to empty and clean them. In Hindu households this was a job for untouchables, but Gandhi had come to the conclusion that Indians must reject the idea of untouchability. It was too much like the racial prejudice most whites showed toward Indians and Africans. Kasturba was offended at being required to do the work of untouchables. She and Mohandas had a bitter argument but in the end Kasturba took her turn at the job.

Gandhi had come to feel that learning self-reliance was more important than formal education. He would not send his sons to local schools because he felt they were too European. The instruction was only in English and Gandhi was afraid the boys would learn Western ways without learning anything of their own culture. Even though he made them wear Western clothes, especially shoes that hurt their feet, he kept them at home hoping to find the time to tutor them himself. When they were grown, all four of Gandhi's sons resented the fact that he had prevented them from getting good educations.

In 1899, war broke out between the British and Boer settlers in South Africa. The source of the trouble was in the Transvaal, where the Dutch farmers were angry with English adventurers who were moving into Boer territory to mine gold and diamonds. Personally, Gandhi was for the Boers but he felt obligated to serve with the British. He stated that citizens of the empire had to support the government from which they expected benefits. He also thought it would be a fine political opportunity to earn improved conditions for Indians by demonstrating loyalty to the empire. Gandhi believed that all war is immoral so, instead of forming an Indian regiment to kill enemy soldiers, he decided to establish an Indian ambulance corps of stretcher-bearers and hospital workers. Gandhi and some others began training as nurses but because of racial prejudice, the Natal government would not permit them to serve. Then

Indian Ambulance Corps organized by Gandhi on the outbreak of the Boer War.

the war began to get difficult for the British, and the corps was allowed to go into action. They were especially heroic at one of the bloodiest fights in the war, the Battle of Spion Kop. The young newspaper correspondent Winston Churchill was also at Spion Kop but Gandhi did not meet him until a few years later in London. Gandhi won a medal for his service at Spion Kop.

When the war was over, Gandhi thought his work in Natal was finished. The task of improving the situation of Indians in South Africa could be carried on by friends. Furthermore, Gandhi hoped that Indian loyalty to the empire during the crisis of war would be

Spion Kop, site of a major battle of the Boer War

rewarded with better treatment. He got ready to move his family back to Bombay, where he intended to open a law office and enter politics. Farewell gifts of gold, silver, and diamonds were showered upon the family. This made Gandhi most uncomfortable because he believed that "a public worker should accept no costly gifts." He decided to refuse the treasures, but Kasturba did not want to part with a very expensive gold necklace.

Harilal, Ramdas, Kasturba, Devadas, and Manilal about 1901.

Kasturba, Gandhi's loyal wife, was by his side for sixty-two years.

"What right have you to my necklace?" she wept.

"Is the necklace given you for your service or for my service?" answered Mohandas.

"I have toiled . . . for you day and night. Is that no service?" replied Kasturba.

Without his wife's hard work and loyal support, Gandhi could not have carried on his own work. Nevertheless, she could not convince him to see her point. All gifts were deposited in a bank as a trust fund to supply money for community service.

Back in India, Gandhi made new political ties with the Indian National Congress. The Congress, as it came to be called, was founded in 1885 by an Englishman named Allan Octavian Hume. Its original purpose was to serve as a forum where educated, English-speaking Indians could voice their opinions about the British government of India. At first the organization, which had British approval, was loyal to the empire. Later, as more and more Indians became westernized and entered the professions and business, the Congress began to demand legal reform and a greater say in local government. Eventually it would become a major force in driving the British out of India, and today it is a major political party in independent India. In 1902, when Gandhi was making his connections in the Congress, he was coached by his friend and mentor Gokhale.

The new career was hardly begun, however, before Gandhi was called back to South Africa in November 1902. The government in England was extremely anxious to keep peace between the British and the Boers in the newly formed Union of South Africa. Many concessions were granted and a former Boer leader, General Louis

Botha, became prime minister. His government was determined to "drive the coolies out of the country." Secretary of State for the Colonies Joseph Chamberlain would be visiting from London, and the Indian community in South Africa wanted Gandhi to meet with him in Durban. They hoped he could persuade Mr. Chamberlain to do something about the rising tide of racial prejudice.

Chamberlain, who had other issues on his mind, was only mildly sympathetic. He told Gandhi the Indians would have to try and make their own peace with the Europeans if they wanted to live

The Right Hon. Secretary of State for the Colonies Joseph Chamberlain.

Johannesburg about 1900.

among them. Gandhi saw that the situation was much worse than he had thought. The Indians' ambulance service during the Boer War was totally forgotten. Indians who had fled the Transvaal during the war were not allowed to return to their homes and businesses. Indians who wanted to cross the border between Natal and the Transvaal had to have a special permit, which was not easy to obtain. Gandhi wangled one, using old connections, and went to study the conditions in Johannesburg. The new Asiatic Department, made up entirely of British civil servants, told him that they were looking after Indian matters. They said he was not needed and tried to get him to leave the Transvaal. Instead, Gandhi made plans to establish a new law office in Johannesburg and eventually send for Kasturba and the boys.

In February 1904, pneumonic plague broke out in the Indian section of Johannesburg. This disease attacks the lungs and kills quickly. It is also very contagious, but Gandhi had no fear of it. Along with a few volunteers, he nursed some of the sickest patients in an old building at the edge of town. The health authorities evacuated everyone from the ghetto and relocated them in tents outside the city. Then, to wipe out the plague, they set fire to all the buildings in "the coolie location."

One of the volunteers who had appeared during the crisis was an Englishman named Albert West. He ran a printing shop and Gandhi thought the man might be more useful as the manager of the weekly newspaper *Indian Opinion.* The paper had been founded in Durban by Gandhi to communicate with the Indians of South Africa. It was printed in English and three Indian languages, Hindi, Tamil, and Gujarati. Gandhi intended the articles and editorials to educate Indians about their political cause, but the paper discussed other matters as well. It contained information about how Indians could improve their diet, sanitary habits, and daily living. But *Indian Opinion* was in chaos. When West arrived in Durban he discovered that the editor was about to depart for India, leaving the accounts in a mess and the bills unpaid. West reported the situation to Gandhi, who promptly boarded a train for Durban to help straighten out the affairs of the paper.

On the twenty-four-hour trip, Gandhi read a small book called *Unto This Last*. It was a collection of essays by the English writer and art critic John Ruskin, who believed that true wealth was not in money. He thought possessions and power should be discarded and rich and poor alike should devote themselves to self-possession and peace. Gandhi interpreted this to mean that a simple life of labor, farming, and craftsmanship was the only life worth living. He arrived in Durban with an exciting idea churning in his mind.

John Ruskin,
English writer.

Gandhi thought that perhaps he could turn *Indian Opinion* into a model of the simple life. He bought a ninety-acre farm outside Durban near a town called Phoenix and moved the paper there. There were a few rocky areas, lots of snakes, and no buildings, but the soil was rich and there was a good orchard. Living in tents, with a corrugated iron shed for the printing press, Gandhi and West developed a self-sufficient community where the staff farmed the land, edited the paper, and ran the presses. Phoenix Settlement was the first of several communities, or ashrams, Gandhi founded in South Africa and India.

Actually, Gandhi did not spend much time on the farm, as he had to get back to his law office in Johannesburg. In 1905, Kasturba and the three youngest sons, Manilal, Ramdas, and Devadas, joined him from India. They lived in a large rented house with most of the staff from the law office. The practice was quite successful and Gandhi was becoming a rich man. Most people would be more than satisfied to become successful and wealthy before reaching middle age, but Gandhi was restless. He continued to work for the welfare of Indians in South Africa. He wrote petitions to the government and editorials for *Indian Opinion* and gave many speeches. One aim of his work was to convince Indians to be more sanitary in the management of their households. He urged this for better community health and so that Indians might be more acceptable to non-Indians. However, no one seemed to be responding to Gandhi's flood of words. In his frustration he began to look for ways to change his life.

In 1906, the Zulu Rebellion broke out in Natal. Actually, it was not an organized rebellion but a series of violent incidents sparked when a Zulu chief killed a tax collector. The British authorities launched an expedition of local volunteer troops to punish the Zulus. As he had during the Boer War, Gandhi formed an Indian volunteer ambulance corps. The amateur soldiers began putting down the so-called rebellion by locking up a lot of unarmed Zulu farmers in a stockade and flogging them. Sergeant Major Gandhi and his ambulance corps set up a hospital to clean and bandage the festering wounds of the innocent tribesmen. Then the corps accompanied the troops on long marches into the hills, where the soldiers flogged and shot any Zulus they found. The brutality of the expedition caused such a scandal that it was called off in a few weeks. Later, in his autobiography, Gandhi wrote that his heart was with the Zulus. "But I then believed that the British Empire existed for the welfare of the world."

During the dusty marches and cold nights Gandhi had plenty of time to think about his future. He came to the conclusion that he had to eliminate all distractions and devote his life totally to public service. This would require discipline and concentration. He decided to take the ancient Hindu vow of self-control called *brahmacharya,* which is intended to force all human emotions, energies, and desires inward to build up spiritual strength. To achieve this Gandhi swore to be modest in speaking and eating, and to refrain forever from hatred, anger, and sex. In addition, to avoid the diversions of wealth and comfort, he decided to give up the affluent life in Johannesburg and take his family to Phoenix Settlement in Natal. First, however, Gandhi had to help deal with new trouble brewing in the Transvaal.

The government in Johannesburg had proposed a law called the

Asiatic Registration Bill. This would require all Indians and Chinese in the Transvaal to be fingerprinted like criminals and to carry certificates of registration at all times. Those who failed to comply with this law would be sent to prison, fined, or deported. Gandhi thought that if it became law, the "Black Act" would lead to even more discrimination and "absolute ruin for the Indians of South Africa." He arranged to have the chairman of the British–Indian Association of the Transvaal call a mass meeting at the Empire Theatre in Johannesburg. Three thousand angry Indians listened to the chairman read a resolution asking Hindus and Muslims alike to refuse to register. Other speakers urged everyone present to pledge refusal. Gandhi rose to remind the audience that a pledge was serious business. It was easy to make in the excitement of the moment but was everyone ready to accept the risks of jail, beatings, and perhaps death? "Everyone must search only his own heart," said Gandhi, "and if the inner voice assures him he has the requisite strength . . . then only should he pledge himself. . . ." After he finished, the entire multitude rose and swore to disobey the law even if it meant going to jail. Then they sang the British Empire anthem, "God Save the King."

The pledge was a new kind of opposition to government unfairness. Many people described it as "passive resistance." To Gandhi, this term included the possibility of hatred "and it could finally manifest itself as violence." As a Hindu, Gandhi was deeply committed to the doctrine of *ahimsa*, or nonviolence. He wanted to show the world that the pledge at the Empire Theatre was a form of quiet opposition based on truth and love. In *Indian Opinion* he offered a prize for anyone who could think of a good name for the new concept. At Phoenix Settlement, a cousin, Maganlal Gandhi, won the prize with *sadagraha* which, in Hindi, means "firmness in a good cause." Mohandas refined the new word to *satyagraha*, adding truth and love to the idea of firmness. Gandhi spent the rest of his life refining and illustrating the meaning of satyagraha.

In an effort to strengthen the case of the Indians and satyagraha, Gandhi took a delegation to England to persuade the British government to withhold approval of the law. As a Crown Colony, the Transvaal had to have royal assent for any new legislation. During October of 1906, Gandhi met with many very important officials, including Prime Minister Sir Henry Campbell-Bannerman. One of the officials he spoke with was Under-Secretary of State for the Colonies Winston Churchill. Some years later, Churchill would make some rude remarks about Gandhi, but this interview went well. Churchill pointed out that, by previous agreement, the Transvaal would be granted self-government as of January 1907. Without the need for royal assent, what would prevent them from passing even worse laws than the Asiatic Registration Bill? Gandhi replied that no law could be worse. The only meeting that ever took place between the two men ended with Churchill cheerfully promising to help as much as he could.

On the way back to South Africa, Gandhi and his friends learned that Secretary of State for the Colonies Victor Alexander Bruce, Lord Elgin, had refused assent for the Black Act. To the Indians of South Africa it seemed as though Gandhi had won a great victory. Early in 1907, however, the bill was reintroduced and in July it became law. At first the government was reluctant to arrest resisters and kept postponing the deadline for registration.

Under-Secretary of State
for the Colonies
Winston Churchill.

Finally, they began making arrests, and in January 1908 Gandhi was brought into court. He asked for the worst punishment allowed since he knew the law and had deliberately broken it. The puzzled judge said that simple admission of guilt did not necessarily call for the maximum punishment. Instead of the allowable six months in prison and a fine, he sentenced Gandhi to two months in prison without a fine. It was the first experience Gandhi had with what he called "His Majesty's Hotels." He soon learned to use the time to catch up on his reading, which included the Gita, the Koran, and the Bible. He also read an essay called "Civil Disobedience" by the American writer Henry David Thoreau. Some people say that this is where Gandhi got his concept of nonviolent opposition. He was certainly impressed with Thoreau's essay but he did not read it until he had been thrown into jail for practicing his own form of civil disobedience. The fact is that Thoreau probably got some of his ideas from reading the Bhagavad Gita and the Upanishads, Hindu sacred literature with which Gandhi had grown up.

The jails were filling up and former Boer general Jan Christiaan Smuts, now minister in charge of Indian affairs, suggested a compromise. He would release the prisoners if they would register voluntarily. Then he would repeal the law. Gandhi accepted. Many Indians thought this was a betrayal and when Gandhi went to register, he was beaten up by some of them. The resistance continued and the government used this as an excuse to withhold the legal appeal to repeal the act. At a mass meeting in Johannesburg, more than two thousand Satyagrahis burned their registration certificates. Gandhi and many others were put back in jail. When they finished their sentences they would agitate against the law again, and again be returned to prison.

By late spring of 1909 the situation had become a stalemate. In a final effort to resolve the issue, Gandhi led a delegation to London to lobby for the repeal of the Black Act. They spent three months discussing their cause in many meetings with government officials and influential private citizens. Gandhi also met with several Indian nationalists who started him thinking about the possibility of Indian independence. By November it was clear the British government was not prepared to offer any help, so the delegation sailed for home. At sea Gandhi wrote a booklet called *Hind Swaraj or Indian Home Rule.* For nine days he wrote feverishly in Gujarati on ship's stationery and when his right hand got tired, he switched to his left. The essay's theme was the struggle of the ancient Indian civilization against modern industrialized civilization. Gandhi regarded the Indian civilization as superior because of its focus on spiritual concerns. He regarded the modern as satanic because of its fascination with material things. Gokhale was upset when he first read it and said that Gandhi did not really understand India. In the essay he had idealized ancient India and some of his hopes for the future were impractical. Nevertheless, Gandhi would always regard *Hind Swaraj* as one of his best pieces of writing.

When Gandhi landed in South Africa he was broke and depressed. There was no money left to support the campaign. A telegram from Gokhale in India suddenly offered an unexpected ray of hope. Ratan Jamshed Tata, a wealthy Indian industrialist, would donate twenty-five thousand rupees (then equal to about seven thousand dollars) to the satyagraha movement. Most of the Satyagrahis were poor people who could not support their families for very long if they spent their time protesting. It was decided that this money should go to help families in distress. Many of them needed a place to live and work, so Gandhi decided to set up another community like Phoenix Settlement in Natal. A wealthy architect named Hermann Kallenbach bought a thousand acres outside Johannesburg and gave the land to Gandhi in May 1910. The new place was called Tolstoy Farm after the Russian Leo Tolstoy, whose writings on nonviolence and Christ-like living Gandhi admired.

In October 1912, Gokhale arrived in South Africa to study the problems of Indians living there. He came with official rank because he was a member of the Council of the Viceroy of India.

Leo Tolstoy,
Russian writer.

The South African government ministers were impressed. They helped Gandhi arrange a grand tour of Indian communities throughout the country. Even though he was suffering from severe diabetes, Gokhale managed to survive a few days of the rough conditions on Tolstoy Farm. At the end of his tour he conferred with Louis Botha and Jan Christiaan Smuts. After the meeting Gokhale reported to Gandhi that the Asiatic Registration Bill, the cruel and humiliating Black Act, would be repealed. Gandhi doubted the government would keep its promise. Nevertheless, Gokhale left for home insisting that Gandhi's work in South Africa was done and he should return to India.

As it turned out the tax was not repealed and new injustices were imposed on the Indian community. In 1913, a judge in Natal ruled that only Christian marriages had legal status. At the same time a law was passed called the Union Immigration Restriction

Gokhale, wearing a white scarf, is seated to Gandhi's right at a meeting of Indian leaders in Durban, 1912.

Gen. Jan Christiaan Smuts.

Act, prohibiting future Indian immigration to South Africa. Gandhi now felt it necessary to expand the satyagraha movement from the Transvaal to the whole Union of South Africa. He organized a series of protest marches, hoping to overcrowd the jails with Satyagrahis, including himself, Kasturba, and other members of his own family. He also kept the British government in London and nationalist leaders in India thoroughly informed about the marches and the jailings. Both groups were indignant toward the South African government. In June 1914, Gandhi negotiated with General Smuts.

The result was the Indian Relief Bill, which was passed by the Union Parliament in July. All Hindu and Muslim marriages would be recognized and all unfair taxes on Indians removed, but most of the Union Immigration Restriction Act would remain.

Gandhi regarded the compromise as a victory for satyagraha. He sent General Smuts a present, a pair of sandals he had made while in prison. For twenty-five summers Smuts wore the sandals while working on his farm, Doornkloof. On Gandhi's seventieth birthday in 1939, Smuts returned them saying, "I have worn these sandals . . . even though I may feel that I am not worthy to stand in the shoes of such a man."

*A portrait of Gandhi taken soon after he and Kasturba
returned to India in 1915.*

CHAPTER FOUR

BREAKING WITH BRITAIN

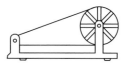

It was time to let the wounds heal. This was the message Gandhi gave to the crowds that greeted him during his farewell tour of South Africa. In July of 1914, he and Kasturba sailed for England to meet with Gokhale. While they were at sea, the First World War broke out and Gokhale returned to India. In London, Gandhi formed an ambulance corps of Indians living in England. Then he came down with pleurisy brought on by breathing the damp winter air. He was advised to seek a warmer climate and in January 1915, Gandhi and Kasturba went home to India.

After visiting relatives in Porbandar, Gandhi went to stay with Gokhale, who was very ill in Pune, a town eighty miles southeast of Bombay. Gokhale was about to die, but before he did he got Gandhi to promise to stay out of politics for one year. Gokhale said Gandhi had lost touch with the Indian people during the years in South Africa and urged him to spend a year of "silence" traveling

The Gandhis at a reception in Gujarat, 1915.

throughout India to refresh his understanding of the people.

Gandhi's first visit was to Santiniketan, or "Home of Peace," in Bengal. Santiniketan was a school dedicated to the arts, founded by the poet Rabindranath Tagore, who had won the 1913 Nobel Prize for Literature. Charles Andrews, an English clergyman who had assisted with Gandhi's work in South Africa, was teaching there and had arranged for about twenty young people from Phoenix Settlement to be guests at the school. These two very different personalities, Tagore and Gandhi, soon came to admire each other and some people say it was Tagore who first called Gandhi "Mahatma," or "Great Soul." They spent time together discussing the future of India and talking with students. Then, while Tagore was away in Calcutta, Gandhi decided to reform the school so it would be like Phoenix Settlement. The students were to do their own cooking, wash their own dishes, and improve the sanitation arrangements. Charlie Andrews objected to such high-handed interference, but Gandhi persisted. When Tagore returned, he found the teachers of Santiniketan in an uproar. A conference was called to restore peace and it was decided that Gandhi and the students from Phoenix Settlement would search for a place to found their own ashram.

Rabindranath Tagore, Indian poet, winner of the 1913 Nobel Prize for Literature.

After many potential sites were considered, Satyagraha Ashram was finally founded in the village of Kochrab near the ancient city of Ahmedabad, capital of Gujarat. In modern times, the city on the banks of the Sabarmati River had become an industrial center for textile factories. The major activity of the new community was weaving cloth by hand. More important, Gandhi insisted that untouchables must be accepted into the ashram. When a small family of untouchables arrived, the other ashramites ignored them. Because of her traditional caste upbringing, Kasturba threatened to leave, and the textile manufacturers of Ahmedabad withdrew their financial support. Just when Gandhi had decided he would have to move the ashram, an anonymous donor gave him enough money to support the community for one year, long enough for it to become self-supporting. Later, the donor turned out to be Ambalal Sarabhai, the leading textile manufacturer of Ahmedabad.

After a meeting of the Indian National Congress in 1916, a poor indigo farmer from the village of Champaran came to see Gandhi. He represented thousands of tenant farmers and he had a harsh tale to tell. Cloth dyers would no longer buy the blue dye made from indigo because a cheaper synthetic dye had been invented. Nevertheless, the English landlords still wanted the profits they had made from indigo crops, so they made the farmers pay rents in cash instead of indigo. Gandhi had never even heard of Champaran and knew nothing about indigo plantations. He thought he would not be much use, but the persistent peasant finally persuaded Gandhi to visit and see the injustice for himself.

When Gandhi got to Champaran in the far north of India near the Himalaya Mountains, he saw that the peasants were much too poor to take their case to court. The whole system of tenants and rents would have to be reformed. He sent people out to gather the details of the farmers' grievances. Gandhi himself wanted to hear the landlords' side but they informed him he was a troublemaker who had no business in the area. The local authorities ordered him to leave the district. He refused and was arrested. In court he stated that he had no wish to disobey the law but he owed "obedience to the higher law of our being, the voice of conscience." Before he could be sentenced to prison, higher-ranking British officials dropped the charges and allowed Gandhi to return to his work. They were afraid that if Gandhi were punished, he would become a hero to the peasants. In fact, he already was a hero, and the viceroy, the British ruler of India, set up a committee that included Gandhi to investigate conditions in Champaran. The farmers were awarded partial repayment. Peaceful civil disobedience had triumphed. It was India's first experience of satyagraha in action.

Late in 1917, Gandhi was called back to Ahmedabad to help settle a dispute between the owners of the textile mills and the ten thousand workers who labored in them. Most of them were peasants from nearby rural villages who now found themselves crowded into ghettos and living on starvation wages. They had no official union to protect them but they were just well enough organized to demand a 50-percent pay raise. The mill owners refused any increase in pay. In February 1918, the workers went on strike. They marched through the streets every day and the mill owners felt it necessary to protect their property with armed guards.

Most of the owners, especially Ambalal Sarabhai, were friends of Gandhi, but when he studied the situation he decided the workers were right. He urged them to remain peaceful but persistent. He made them promise that none of them would return to the factories until they were offered a raise. The strikers were nearly starving and many were tempted to go back to work anyway. To encourage them, Gandhi held a meeting every day under a huge tree by the Sabarmati River. "They attended the meeting in their thousands," he wrote, "and I reminded them in my speeches of their pledge and of the duty to maintain peace and self-respect." By March of 1918, he noticed that the crowds forming at the "Keep the Pledge Tree" were much smaller than they had been. Some of the workers were beginning to resent Gandhi. They thought he had nothing to lose while they had everything to lose. To introduce a new element to the deadlock, Gandhi announced, "Unless the strikers . . . continue the strike until a settlement is reached, or unless they leave the mills altogether, I will not touch any food." He had challenged the strikers to continue, but he had also challenged his friends the mill owners to negotiate. After three days of fasting, the strike was ended with an agreement for a 35-percent pay raise. It was the first time Gandhi used fasting in a public cause.

At the same time Gandhi was helping the mill workers, he was coping with another problem at home. Plague had broken out in Kochrab shortly after Gandhi returned to the ashram. In his autobiography he wrote, "It was impossible to keep ourselves immune from the effects of the surrounding insanitation, however scrupulously we might observe the rules of cleanliness within the Ashram walls." Unable to persuade the villagers to adopt good sanitary procedures and afraid for the health of the children in the ashram, Gandhi decided to move it to a location on the Sabarmati River.

The Sabarmati Ashram is now a museum and is often visited by Indian school classes.

One of the crops grown at the new Sabarmati Ashram was cotton, which was hand woven into a coarse cloth called *khadi*. Gandhi's idea was to avoid buying the more expensive cotton woven in England and also to encourage a village industry so Indian peasants could try to pull themselves out of poverty. He decided to create even more self-sufficiency by hand spinning of cotton yarn. He knew nothing about spinning, but a wealthy widow located an antique portable spinning wheel, or *charkha*, and he began to learn. In time, caps and shirts made of khadi became a sort of rough uniform for Gandhi's followers. The rhythmic hum of charkhas became heard all over India, and Gandhi used his own wheel to make a sort of soothing music for meditation in his simple study at Sabarmati.

Making spinning wheels in the shop at Sabarmati Ashram

Gandhi's study at Sabarmati Ashram.

A flickering hope that Dominion status for India might be negotiated after World War I was snuffed out in 1919 when the viceroy's government in Delhi passed the Rowlatt Act. The bill was named for the English judge who had headed the advisory commission that recommended the legislation. It imposed extremely severe punishments on political activity opposed to the government. Gandhi thought the law imposed such unfair restrictions "that no self-respecting people could submit to them." Although he was seriously ill at the time, he campaigned against the bill for months before it was actually passed. His secretary, Mahadev Desai, read Gandhi's speeches calling for a satyagraha campaign. When the bill was about to be passed, Gandhi called for a peaceful general strike called a *hartal*. All Indians across the country would stop work for a day of fasting and prayer to call attention to their humiliation. In some places the demonstrations were peaceful, but there was serious rioting in Delhi. Gandhi took a train from Bombay to Delhi, where he hoped to quell the riots. Government officials thought he would only make matters worse so they had him arrested halfway along the line. He was returned to Bombay and released. Realizing he had made a "Himalayan miscalculation," Gandhi called off the hartal. Satyagraha had failed because it had inspired violence.

The cancellation of the hartal came too late to prevent a horrible tragedy in Amritsar, a northern city that was the scene of some of the worst rioting. Brigadier General Reginald Dyer was sent to restore order and prevent further violence. His first act was to forbid public meetings, but the order was not read where many people would hear it. A crowd of six thousand peaceful and unarmed peasants gathered in a public square called Jallianwala Bagh to celebrate a traditional festival. General Dyer thought the event was a deliberate challenge to his order. He planned to disperse the crowd by sending two armored cars and a column of ninety soldiers through the middle of the square. When he discovered that the streets of Amritsar were too narrow to allow his vehicles into Jallianwala Bagh, he marched in with just the troops. To General Dyer, the peasants in front of him seemed hostile, so he ordered the troops to spread out and fire into the crowd. Ten minutes later there were 379 dead and about 1200 wounded. Six months later, a commission of inquiry made up of four Englishmen and three Indians condemned the actions of General Dyer. He was relieved of his command and sent home to England, but the Indian people never forgot Jallianwala Bagh. Twelve years later, the American journalist Louis Fischer asked Gandhi if he still had faith in the British. He replied, "I had faith in them until 1919. But the Amritsar Massacre . . . changed my heart."

Gandhi was incapable of hatred, but after the massacre, he no longer believed in the benevolence of the British Empire. In November of 1919, Gandhi found a peaceful way to express his newfound opposition. He was invited to attend a Muslim conference in Delhi for the purpose of planning agitation against the breakup of the Turkish Empire in the peace negotiations following World War I. The sultan of Turkey was also the caliph, or head of the Muslim religion. Indian Muslims were very upset that the two holy cities in Arabia, Mecca and Medina, would no longer be ruled by the caliph. It did not matter to Indian Muslims that the Arab Muslims wanted to be free of Turkish rule. The Indians were afraid the caliph was losing Muslim power. Gandhi also did not give much thought to the Arab point of view. He thought mostly about swaraj, self-rule. To achieve this he felt the Hindus and Muslims of India had to join together in a movement of "noncooperation."

To begin with, Gandhi asked that all honors conferred on Indians by the British Empire be returned. He himself returned the medals he had been awarded for his work in the Boer War and the Zulu Rebellion. In addition, the plan called for all lawyers and government officials to stop work and for students to boycott government-funded schools. Indian soldiers in the army were to return their arms, and citizens were to stop paying taxes. Gandhi hoped that the government would be brought to a standstill. Unemployed

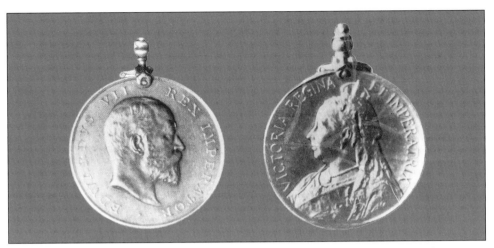

The two medals Gandhi returned to the British government after the Amritsar Massacre of 1919. The one on the left, with a portrait of King Edward VII, was awarded for work in the Zulu Rebellion. The one on the right was for ambulance work in the Boer War.

lawyers, teachers, and students might then create so much political pressure on the British Empire that it would have to grant swaraj within the year.

The population of India was so huge that Gandhi could not manage this scheme all by himself. To meet the needs, a wily old politician named Vallabhbhai Patel helped expand the Indian National Congress in 1920. Provincial committees were established to organize the work of noncooperation in towns and villages throughout India. At the same time, Gandhi began traveling to take the message to all districts. While he traveled he wrote articles for each issue of *Young India*, a weekly newspaper he had founded in 1919. Everywhere he went he attracted wildly enthusiastic crowds. Wherever he stopped, people made huge piles of European-style clothing. Some even stripped themselves naked as a symbol of discarding British tyranny. Then Gandhi would set fire to the towering heap of Western garments. In a sense, he had started India's spirit burning and the people practically worshiped him for it. Rabindranath Tagore and Charlie Andrews, however, criticized the burnings as a form of violence.

Burning foreign cloth.

In April 1921, a new viceroy arrived in India. Rufus Daniel Isaacs, Lord Reading, former ambassador to Washington, D.C., was a brilliant lawyer who had first earned his living as a fruit merchant. One of his first priorities was to arrange a series of meetings with Gandhi. The two men had six conferences in May. Afterward, Lord Reading wrote to his son that Gandhi's "religious and moral views are admirable . . . though I must confess that I find it difficult to understand his practice of them in politics." Lord Reading could not comprehend the Mahatma's fervent belief that "nonviolence and love" would free India. On the other hand, Gandhi was unable to see that his peaceful plans could easily slip out of control and degenerate into fire and bloodshed. There were many leaders who would have preferred to challenge the British Empire with violence. But all leaders knew that the Mahatma seemed like a holy person to millions of Indian peasants and so they bowed to his ideas.

In July and August Gandhi crisscrossed India, always wearing khadi clothing and traveling in third-class railway compartments to emphasize his identity with the poor. Everywhere he carried his message he was greeted by hysterical crowds. He knew that millions of these peasants could not afford to buy substitutes for the garments they threw on his bonfires of foreign clothing. "Let them be satisfied with a mere loin cloth," he urged in *Young India*. To lead the way, Gandhi would do likewise. He stripped away his cap, long vest, and loose trousers and took to wearing nothing but a sort of baggy loincloth called a dhoti and sandals. He carried a cloth bag that held writing materials, nuts, dried fruit, and a rosary. In cold weather he wore a shawl around his shoulders, and in hot sunny weather, a small cloth was sometimes draped over his bald head. The costume was a sharp contrast to the dandified clothing of his early student days in London or even the starched collar and pinstriped suit of his years as a lawyer in South Africa.

The Mahatma's new garb might also have been a startling contrast to the pomp and glitter of the royal visit of the Prince of Wales, who arrived in Bombay in November. Gandhi, however, was in another part of the city, where he had organized a different sort of ceremony. A huge bonfire of foreign clothing was lit to attract crowds away from the prince's arrival. The only people who greeted the royal entourage were Eurasians and others who did not feel included in the national movement. These people were attacked in the name of Mahatma Gandhi by young people wearing khadi. Soon bloody riots broke out. Trolley cars and shops were set on fire. The Mahatma rode around Bombay in a car begging the mobs to stop, but they had worked themselves into a frenzy of destruction. They could no longer hear the voice of reason. Gandhi blamed himself for failing to control the spirit of revolt he had created. "I must do penance for it," he wrote in *Young India*. "I propose henceforth to observe, every Monday, a twenty-four-hours' fast till Swaraj is obtained." Mondays also became days of silence and rest when, if he had to communicate, it was only by means of hand written notes.

The Mahatma still continued to have faith in nonviolent non-cooperation. He thought it might work if it could be very tightly controlled. In spite of the objections of the Congress leaders, who wanted a nationwide campaign, he decided to limit the first campaign of noncooperation to the small territory of Bardoli, a district near Bombay. He hoped that a well-disciplined and peaceful effort would avoid the rioting and bloodshed that had happened in Bombay during the royal visit. It might also serve as an example to persuade Great Britain of India's determined opposition. The government could not throw thousands of people in jail all at once, and it certainly could not kill them. Speaking at the Congress meeting in December 1921, Gandhi issued a warning to the British. "Take care what you are doing," he said, "and see that you do not make the three hundred millions of India your eternal enemies."

A gathering of the Indian National Congress, early 1920s.

From London in January 1922 the secretary of state for the colonies had sent the viceroy instructions to have Gandhi arrested. Lord Reading delayed on the grounds that, although the Mahatma had announced plans for noncooperation, he had not yet actually done anything. So far, there was no action to justify arrest.

The campaign of noncooperation was set to begin on February 8, 1922. On that very day Gandhi learned that a ghastly event had taken place eight hundred miles away in a village called Chauri Chaura. On February 5, a nonviolent procession had marched by the police station. The police let them go in peace but then got into a scuffle with some stragglers. The stragglers called for help and the marchers returned. The twenty-three policemen fired their guns over the heads of the angry mob until their ammunition ran out. They then took refuge in the police station and the mob set it on fire. As the police ran out of the fire they were hacked to pieces and the bloody fragments were thrown back into the fire. The news made Gandhi sick. He called off the campaign in Bardoli and began a five-day fast saying, "I must undergo a personal cleansing."

To the dismay of the leaders of the Congress, the noncooperation movement had been stalled by the Mahatma himself. He was no longer as powerful and popular as he had been. British officials in England and India decided they could now put Gandhi behind bars without risking a bloody protest throughout the country. He was arrested quietly at Sabarmati on the night of March 10, 1922. The trial, which began on March 18, was a remarkably peaceful event. At the opening the judge bowed to Gandhi, and the Mahatma bowed in return. Gandhi had no lawyers and he pleaded guilty to three counts of sedition. The judge granted Gandhi permission to read to the court a long statement he had prepared. Before he began, Gandhi accepted full responsibility for the recent acts of violence. "I know that I was playing with fire," he said. "I do not ask for mercy. . . . I am here, therefore, to invite and cheerfully submit to the highest penalty that can be inflicted upon me. . . ." The Mahatma then read aloud how earlier in his life he had been loyal to Great Britain in the hope that India could "gain a status of full equality in the Empire." Following the Rowlatt Act and "the massacre at Jallianwala Bagh and . . . public flogging and other indescribable humiliations," he lost that hope. He had come to the unhappy conclusion that British law in India existed to exploit the masses. No attempt to justify that law could possibly "explain away the evidence that the skeletons in many villages present to the naked eye." Gandhi believed the law itself was evil and the judge had a simple choice. If he agreed that the law was evil, he must resign. If he believed the system was good for the people, he had to impose the severest penalty possible.

The judge replied that he appreciated the fact that the Mahatma was regarded by millions as a saintly leader. His own job, however, was to judge Gandhi only "as a man subject to the law, who by his own admission has broken the law. . . ." Gandhi was sentenced to six years in prison. He accepted gracefully saying, "So far as the whole proceedings are concerned, I must say that I could not have expected greater courtesy."

The Sabarmati River viewed from a garden at the ashram.

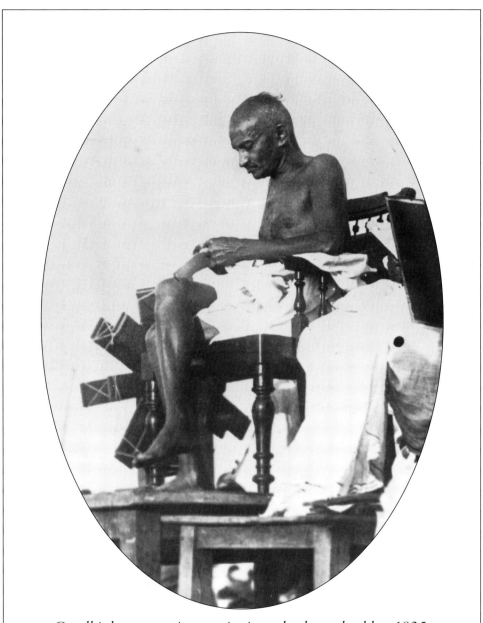

Gandhi demonstrating a spinning wheel, or charkha, 1925.

CHAPTER FIVE

SALT AND
SATYAGRAHA

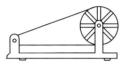

Two years after going to prison, Gandhi sat, wrapped in a shawl, on a long sandy beach near Bombay and stared at the ocean. In prison he had come down with acute appendicitis, which required an emergency operation. Complications slowed his recovery and the British authorities thought it wise to free him. He would recuperate faster at his friend's estate by the sea. Also, the British feared that if the Mahatma happened to die in prison, there would be violence throughout India. Gandhi did not feel entirely ready for his unexpected freedom. In prison he had settled into a regulated life of reading and study. The noncooperation campaign was stalled. Tensions between Hindus and Muslims were rising again. The hope of swaraj seemed like a dream of the past. As he sat on the beach Gandhi sadly pondered the difficulties of starting the movement all over again.

Swaraj seemed impossible unless Hindus and Muslims stood

shoulder to shoulder. Instead, they glowered face-to-face over ancient issues such as Muslims killing cows that were sacred to Hindus or Hindus making festival music that disturbed the religious peace of Muslim mosques. Now a new issue made the tension worse. Muslims were finding it difficult to compete for the lower-level government jobs permitted to Indians. They wanted a certain percentage of these posts to be reserved for Muslims, whether or not they were qualified for the work. The better-educated Hindus could not agree to this. Acts of violence increased. Gandhi was in Delhi when he received horrifying reports of rioting, massacre, and burning in Kohat, on the Northwest Frontier. Feeling a responsibility for having helped to arouse the spirit of the nation, the Mahatma decided to do penance by fasting for twenty-one days.

Gandhi said his decision was private. "My fast is a matter between God and myself," he wrote in an article for *Young India*. It was also a very public scolding. "To revile one another's religion," Gandhi wrote in the same article, "to break the heads of innocent men, to desecrate temples or mosques is a denial of God. The world is watching." The fast, which took place in the house of a Muslim friend, was reported by every newspaper and radio station in India. Charlie Andrews hurried from Santiniketan to act as editor of *Young India*. Many visitors, both Muslim and Hindu, came to see the Mahatma. The sips of water that he allowed himself from time to time were barely enough to sustain his frail body, which was still weak from the ordeal of illness and surgery. On the twelfth day, his doctors thought he would die, but the next day he brightened. On the twenty-first day, Gandhi called a few friends to his side for a simple ceremony. A Muslim leader, or imam, recited

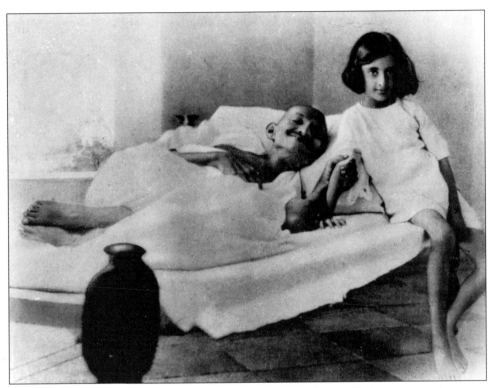

Jawaharlal Nehru's daughter, Indira, was one of Gandhi's many visitors during the Great Fast of 1924. Both father and daughter would later become prime ministers of independent India.

the opening verses of the Koran; Charlie Andrews sang one of the Mahatma's favorite Christian hymns that begins, "When I survey the wondrous cross"; a Hindu follower of Gandhi, Vinobha Bhave, recited holy verses from the Upanishads; and the group sang a Hindu hymn. Gandhi spoke a few faint words in which he called for a promise of Hindu–Muslim unity. Then he drank some orange juice. Mahatma Gandhi had broken his fast.

For the time being, there was peace between Hindus and

Muslims. Gandhi returned to the warmth of Sabarmati Ashram, where he was known lovingly as "Bapu," or Father. Kasturba was called "Ba." The love given and returned in Gandhi's ashram family did not flow as freely with his personal family. The eldest son, Harilal, who had fled from the family when he did not measure up to his father's wishes, was now involved in a very shaky business deal. In *Young India,* Gandhi warned against doing business with Harilal. "Men may be good, not necessarily their children," he concluded.

At Sabarmati, Kasturba was called "Ba," meaning mother.

In 1925, a most unusual disciple arrived. Madeleine Slade, the daughter of a British admiral, had learned of the Mahatma and came to sit at his feet. Gandhi gave her the Indian name Mirabehn and said that she would be his daughter. She became one of his several assistants when he traveled and she often made speeches about satyagraha and the importance of the charkha and khadi.

The Great Fast of 1924 had briefly shocked the nation into peace, but it did not last. It was already unraveling in 1926 when the distinguished and liberal-minded Edward F. L. Wood, Lord Irwin, was appointed as the new viceroy. In that same year Gandhi began what he called his year of silence in response to the growing disunity he saw among the Indian people. Except for his regular totally silent Mondays, Gandhi was anything but silent. The Mahatma's "silence" was simply to refrain from making any comments on the sad confusion he saw spreading over India. Once more there was tension between Hindus and Muslims. The Muslims, fearing that total independence from Britain would leave them at the mercy of the Hindu majority, were forming their own organization. It was called the Muslim League and its most prominent leader was a man called Mohamed Ali Jinnah. The Congress, now sometimes referred to as the Congress Party, was fragmenting into factions, none of which seemed to believe in nonviolence.

In February 1928, a delegation made up of seven members of the English Parliament arrived in Bombay. The group was led by Sir John Simon and its task was to study the Indian governmental system in order to recommend possible changes to the British government. Although it had the power to shape the affairs of India, there was not a single Indian on the Simon Commission. No insult could

have inspired greater noncooperation. The Commission was greeted everywhere by crowds waving black flags and chanting "Simon,
go back." The Congress Party and the Muslim League, as well as
other Indian political organizations, were invited to help the Simon
Commission in its studies. They all refused. Gandhi said he was not
interested in discussions with the British and stated, "I am concen-
trating my attention upon the means of attainment of swaraj." He
told Charlie Andrews that he did not trust the Simon Commission.

The Congress appointed its own commission led by Motilal

Indians protesting the Simon Commission, 1928.

Nehru, the father of Jawaharlal, who would later become India's first prime minister. Claiming to speak for all Indians, this group set out to write a constitution for an independent India. They neglected to discuss the matter with the Muslim League, and the tensions between Hindus and Muslims increased. Watching the rising tide of unrest all over India, the Mahatma decided that it was time to act. On January 26, 1930, he issued a declaration of independence. It sounded rather like the American Declaration of Independence. He began with the "inalienable right" of people to be free to control their own lives, which is a fundamental concept in the American Declaration. Another right, the "right to alter or abolish" an oppressive government, was described in language that could have been written by Thomas Jefferson himself. In conclusion, Gandhi stated that "the British Government . . . has ruined India economically, politically, culturally and spiritually. We believe, therefore, that India must sever the British connection and attain *Purna Swaraj* or Complete Independence."

Gandhi believed that satyagraha was the only weapon Indians had to wield against the might of the British Empire, and khadi was their uniform. The spinning wheel and home weaving were teaching people to be self-sufficient and therefore no longer dependent on foreign industry. Khadi gave them dignity, but the Mahatma was forced to conclude that its symbolism was still not strong enough to unify all the competing factions. Furthermore, violence was looking more and more attractive to some Indians. The Great Depression, which had been triggered by the Wall Street crash of October 1929, was creating even more economic hardship than usual for most Indians. Gandhi searched his imagination for a new symbol that could electrify the millions of peasants of India into forming a single body of total protest against British rule. He found it in a common and humble commodity: salt.

The British government in India controlled the sale of salt. It was against the law to own salt that had not been processed and sold, at a slight profit, by the government. The salt tax was an issue that had perplexed Gandhi even as long ago as his student days in London. He decided that now was the time to challenge the law.

The Congress did not quite understand the significance of Gandhi's intentions, and it expressed puzzlement. Nevertheless, on March 12, 1930, the Mahatma closed Sabarmati Ashram, announcing he would not return until swaraj was achieved. Along with seventy-eight selected volunteers, he started walking toward Dandi, a town on the seashore two hundred and forty miles to the south. Gandhi was sixty-one years old but he was able to stride along on his pipestem legs as briskly as the youngest member of the group, who was sixteen. They marched an average of twelve miles a day in the scorching Indian sun. At every village they came to they stopped to rest and the Mahatma talked to the people urging them to wear khadi, swear off alcohol, install proper sanitation, and treat untouchables as equals. Young people from each of the villages they visited joined the Satyagrahis, and the ranks eventually swelled to two or three thousand. Throughout the journey Gandhi wrote in his journal and spent an hour a day at his spinning wheel.

The government was just as puzzled as the Congress. Although they were concerned, the officials decided to watch and wait. Perhaps there was little they could do anyway. Not only was all of India also watching and waiting, news correspondents along on the

Beginning the Salt March at Sabarmati, 1930.

march were sending dispatches to newspapers and radio stations all over the world. On the eve of the anniversary of the Amritsar Massacre, the marchers arrived in Dandi. When asked what he hoped to achieve, Gandhi wrote a note that read, "I want world sympathy in this battle of Right against Might." The little army prayed all night and on the morning of April 6, Gandhi went down to the shore to take a ceremonial bath in the sea. As he walked back up the beach, he bent to pick up a small lump of sea salt. The Mahatma had broken the law.

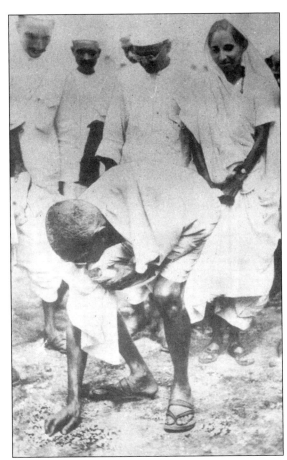

Gandhi picking up salt on the beach at Dandi.

At first there was a stillness all across India. After a few days people began swarming to gather salt all along the thirty-five hundred miles of India's coastline. Inland, everyone was learning to make and sell salt, including members of the Congress. Jawaharlal Nehru, the president of Congress for 1930, wrote in his autobiography, "As we saw the abounding enthusiasm of the people and the way salt-making was spreading like a prairie fire, we felt a little

*Gandhi's note
to a journalist
at Dandi.*

abashed and ashamed for having questioned . . . this method when it was first proposed by Gandhiji." Elsewhere in his book Nehru explains that "*ji* is one of the commonest additions to a name in India. . . . It conveys an idea of respect, something equivalent to Mr., Mrs., or Miss."

By picking up a little piece of salt, Gandhiji, as many were beginning to call him, had given Indians their self-respect. Throughout the country they demonstrated their new strength. People continued to make and sell salt, picket liquor stores, and burn foreign cloth, but the lesson of Chauri Chaura was well remembered. Although people were injured in clashes with the police and some blood was spilled, the challenge to the government remained basically nonviolent.

In those days, Indian women rarely took part in public affairs.

Indian women on their way to Madras beach to gather salt.

Nevertheless, huge numbers of women left their homes to join and sometimes lead the nonviolent marches and picketing. The government felt that order had to be restored. They started arresting Indians involved in protest, including Gandhi's son Devadas, numerous members of Congress, and even Jawaharlal Nehru himself. Nehru's elderly father became president of Congress until he too was arrested. By the end of April, there were approximately sixty thousand men and women crowded in jails throughout India.

Tensions escalated dramatically on April 23, when "the Frontier Gandhi," a Muslim named Khan Abdul Ghaffar Khan, was arrested in Peshawar on the northwestern border. His nonviolent organization called the Red Shirts was remarkable because it was made up of fierce Pathan tribesmen. "The Pathans," wrote Nehru in his autobiography, "noted for their courage, were not noted for their peaceful nature; and these Pathans . . . set an example which was unique in India." They peacefully took over the city and released Ghaffar Khan. Hindu troops from the Garhwali Rifles were sent to

Gandhi with Khan Abdul Ghaffar Khan, "the Frontier Gandhi."

restore order, but they refused to fire on the Muslim crowds. A troop of Gurkhas, fierce Nepalese tribesmen, finally retook the city. The mutiny of the Garhwali Rifles and other acts of military disobedience around the country thoroughly alarmed Lord Irwin. To avoid encouraging further disorder he decided to censor the newspapers.

Gandhi was so upset by the censorship that he sent an angry letter to the viceroy. Behind his anger lay a determination to maintain the challenge. He wanted to force the government to use even tougher methods of control. Then, with the whole world watching, the British might be shamed into leaving India for good. Gandhi informed the viceroy that he intended to lead a group of Satyagrahis in taking over the Dharasana Saltworks, a government-owned facility on the shore, a hundred and fifty miles north of Bombay. The government's response was to arrest the Mahatma under the authority of an outdated statute passed in 1827 when the East India Company was the only British authority in India. He was held at Yeravda Jail in Pune with no trial and no sentence at "the pleasure of the Government." The terms were harsh but, as Gandhi wrote to Mirabehn, he was well treated and "making up for arrears in sleep." He meditated, read books, translated Hindu hymns into English, and worked at his spinning wheel every day.

Turmoil increased all over India. There were many marches on salt depots on the west coast but the one Gandhi had announced before his arrest became famous because he made sure that international journalists would be there. The march was taken over by one of his disciples, the poet Mrs. Sarojini Naidu. She reminded the twenty-five hundred Satyagrahis that, in the tradition of nonvio-

ABOVE: *Yeravda Jail, Pune. Gandhi once gave this as his home address to British authorities.*

LEFT: *Mrs. Sarojini Naidu.*

lence, "you must not even raise a hand to ward off a blow." They gathered a short distance from the four hundred policemen and six British officers who stood guard at the ditches and barbed wire that surrounded the saltworks. A column of Satyagrahis advanced and were met by a group of policemen who started to beat them with steel-tipped bamboo clubs called *lathis*. Webb Miller, an American newspaper correspondent working for United Press International, said that the Satyagrahis did not even lift their arms to protect themselves. "From where I stood," he reported, "I heard the sickening whack of the clubs on unprotected skulls. . . . Those struck down fell sprawling, unconscious or writhing with fractured skulls or broken shoulders." Others still able to stand marched silently on until they too were beaten down. Then another column would form and take the place of the first. Some of the wounded were lucky enough to be carried by volunteer stretcher-bearers to a temporary hospital. More wounded lay on the bloody ground and in the ditches in the 116-degree heat. They were kicked and tortured by the outnumbered police who, by midday, had become panicked and angry.

"I have never witnessed such harrowing scenes as at Dharasana," said Webb Miller who, in his twenty years of reporting, had seen a great deal of brutality. Mirabehn, the English admiral's daughter who had become a Gandhi disciple, was equally stunned when she toured the hospital where bloody and battered bodies groaned in agony. "What has become of English honor," she wrote, "English justice? No amount of argument can excuse what they have been doing at Dharasana." The Mahatma's old colleague Rabindranath Tagore, who had accepted a knighthood from King

George V in 1915 but then renounced the title in 1919 after the Amritsar Massacre, saw the incident as a disgrace not only for England but for all of Europe. "She is no longer regarded as the champion throughout the world of fair dealing," he said in an interview with the *Manchester Guardian,* "but as the upholder of Western race supremacy. . . . For Europe this is, in actual fact, a great moral defeat."

The British were not, however, to be driven out of India immediately. On the other hand, they could not overcome Gandhi. Sitting in Yeravda Jail, he seemed to have a stronger hold on the spirit of India than he did while working in his ashram. In August, the government tried to end the political stalemate by allowing intermediaries to arrange a conference of imprisoned leaders. The two Nehrus, Mrs. Naidu, who had been arrested after the march on the Dharasana Saltworks, plus half a dozen Congress cabinet members were all transported from various prisons to meet with Gandhi at Yeravda Jail. After two days, they concluded that the only solution to the problem was full independence for India. They said that the Congress and the British government were separated by "an unbridgeable gulf."

Lord Irwin was actually a kindly, peaceful, and deeply religious man. As viceroy, he found himself extremely frustrated. Many members of the Labor government back in England favored Indian independence. In spite of his own instincts and the desires of many Englishmen, Lord Irwin found himself thrust unwillingly into directing a campaign of oppression. Further disappointment was created by the failure of the Round Table Conference, which met in London from November 1930 to January 1931. Its purpose was to discuss the possibility of Dominion status for India similar to that enjoyed by other countries within the British Empire such as Canada and Australia. The main reason for failure was that no Congress members had been invited to attend. The only bright spot was in the last session when Prime Minister Ramsay MacDonald hoped there could be a Second Round Table Conference that would include members of the Congress. With this slender encouragement, Lord Irwin decided to try conciliation. He freed Gandhi and more than twenty Congress leaders.

In February, Gandhi agreed to have a series of discussions with Lord Irwin. The viceroy, who was six feet, five inches tall, was curiously impressed by the bald little man who came to his study in the elegant and imposing palace in Delhi wearing a dhoti and shawl. "Small, wizened, rather emaciated, no front teeth," wrote Irwin to King George V, "yet you cannot help feeling the force of character behind the sharp little eyes. . . ." The two men developed a cautious trust of each other. Gandhi talked too much, but the viceroy was extremely patient. Their meetings resulted in a truce that came to be known as the Delhi Pact. Gandhi was to call off the campaign of nonviolent protest and Irwin was to release all Satyagrahis from prison. Limited salt production would be permitted and arrangements would be made for the Second Round Table Conference. It was not a peace treaty but at least it was a bargain struck in good faith.

The delegates to the Second Round Table Conference included Hindus, Muslims, Christians, princes, and landowners. There was no one, however, to represent the millions of peasants and untouchables. The Mahatma appointed himself to the job but this

The Second Round Table Conference, London, 1931.

created resentment later on. The Indian National Congress had decided to appoint Gandhi as their sole representative. Politically, this was not a wise move as one individual alone could not speak for all the constituencies of the Congress. Furthermore, Gandhi was more interested in social issues than he was in politics. Nevertheless, he was cheerful as he boarded a steamer in Bombay on August 29 accompanied by his son Devadas, Mrs. Naidu, Mirabehn, and his secretary, Mahadev Desai. The arrival in London on a chilly September day must have reminded Gandhi of another September arrival forty-three years before. He had been wearing white on that occasion too but it had not been khadi.

Instead of staying at a hotel convenient to the conference meeting place at St. James's Palace in the center of London, Gandhi decided to stay five miles away at a settlement house in a grimy and gritty working-class district. He said he wanted to get to know the people of England. At times that seemed to be his main purpose. He walked the neighborhood near the settlement house to talk with the poor people and their children. He wore his dhoti and shawl to Buckingham Palace to have tea with King George V, who told him, "I won't have you stirring up trouble in my empire." Later, when asked if he hadn't felt scantily clad when meeting the king, Gandhi replied, "The king had on enough for both of us."

King George V.

He traveled out of London to meet famous people, to talk with scholars at Oxford University, and to visit Cambridge, where both Nehru and Charlie Andrews had been students. His most remarkable trip was to Lancashire, where unemployed cotton mill workers greeted "Mr. Gandhi" with warm enthusiasm. These people might have confronted him with hatred, as his khadi program had caused their unemployment by seriously shrinking the market for the cloth they produced. Instead, they adored him for his sympathy toward the working classes.

English mill workers cheering Gandhi in Lancashire, 1931.

Even when he stayed in London for the conference Gandhi's schedule was so busy he slept only two hours a night. It was no wonder his eyes were sometimes closed during long discussions. As the conference turned out, it probably did not matter much that Gandhi failed to give it his full attention and energy. Halfway through it there was an election in England. The Conservatives won in a landslide and, as the Depression deepened, the government ceased to care about Indian independence. On top of that there were so many conflicting desires among the Indian delegates that consensus was impossible. The Second Round Table Conference was a failure. But Gandhi's twelve weeks in England were a publicity success. He gave many speeches, was frequently interviewed, made a radio broadcast to America for CBS, and was often photographed for the newspapers. By being highly visible in London, the little brown man in a loincloth made the issue of swaraj familiar to the English and to world opinion. To Ghanshayam Das Birla, an Indian millionaire at the conference, he remarked that he had only one thing to say: "We want independence." All other questions became insignificant in the face of that three-word statement.

A new viceroy had been appointed by the time Gandhi's ship docked in Bombay on December 28. Freeman Freeman-Thomas, Lord Willingdon, was a strict and rigid administrator who had spent nearly thirty years in colonial government, all but five of them in India. He already had had Nehru and Ghaffar Khan arrested. His reaction to the hero's welcome the Mahatma received was to clap him in jail as soon as possible. Again Gandhi found himself in Yeravda Jail on the authority of the outdated statute of 1827.

Soon all the leaders of Congress were also thrown into prison. During the first two months of 1932, more than thirty thousand people were imprisoned for political reasons.

In prison, Gandhi enjoyed the company of his secretary, Mahadev Desai, and the Congress politician Vallabhbhai Patel. He also read many books, worked at his spinning wheel, and brooded on the issues of the Second Round Table Conference. The one that preoccupied him most was how to choose local and national representation for untouchables under a proposed Indian constitution to be considered at a Third Round Table Conference. He was totally opposed to a suggestion he read about in the newspapers that they should have a specific number of representatives who would be elected solely by untouchables. Gandhi thought this was sure to continue the historic division between caste Hindus and untouchables. They should, he insisted, be included as Hindus in any future form of representative government. He sent a letter to England informing the British government that if they decided to create a separate electorate for the untouchables, he would "fast unto death." He wrote that although his fast would cause "grave embarrassment to His Majesty's Government . . . it is the call of conscience which I dare not disobey."

Most of the people who were close to Gandhi were horrified that he would try to force his will on the government by threatening to fast. They saw it as plain political blackmail. It was several months before the government answered Gandhi. In mid-August 1932, word came that the government had chosen to recognize the untouchables as a minority community entitled to a separate electorate. The Mahatma announced that he would begin his fast on

September 20. Prime Minister MacDonald was puzzled at Gandhi's determination. Like most Englishmen, he did not comprehend the ancient hatred of caste Hindus that was harbored in the hearts of most untouchables. Many of them preferred British rule to the possibility of Hindu rule. Some liked Muslims better than caste Hindus. Gandhi felt that if this deep division within the Hindu community was not healed, swaraj would fail. The issue of the fast was bigger than the voting status of untouchables. Tagore explained the matter to his students at Santiniketan: "The penance which the Mahatmaji has taken upon himself is . . . a message to all India and the world. . . . No civilized society can thrive upon victims. . . . Those whom we keep down inevitably drag us down." Gandhi was protesting the whole concept of untouchability. Newspapers and radios throughout the country made sure that all Indians had to take notice.

The elderly Gandhi was already frail when he began fasting. Near the end of the first week he could not walk, but untouchables all over India were walking freely. Hindu temple doors were opened to them. They were allowed to travel on public roads and draw water at public wells. Various castes shared ceremonial meals with them, and a voting compromise was being negotiated. Kasturba was transferred from her jail at Sabarmati to be with her weakening Bapu at Yeravda. Finally, a complicated proposal, involving many technicalities in addition to primary elections for the untouchables, was sent to London for Cabinet consideration. It was promptly approved and returned. The Mahatma was not entirely happy with some parts of the agreement but realized that any objections might ruin the pact. Reluctantly, he gave his approval. He then accepted a glass of orange juice from Kasturba, and another of his public fasts was ended.

A three-thousand-year-old tradition could not be reversed in a couple of weeks. After a short while, the temple doors were once more closed to untouchables. For the time being, one fifth of the Indian population became outcaste again. It would take much more time to change Hindu attitudes, but Gandhi had started the process. He had established the principle that no one should be treated as untouchable in the new India. If this had been Gandhi's only achievement in life it would have been enough to earn him the title Mahatma.

Entrance to a Hindu temple.

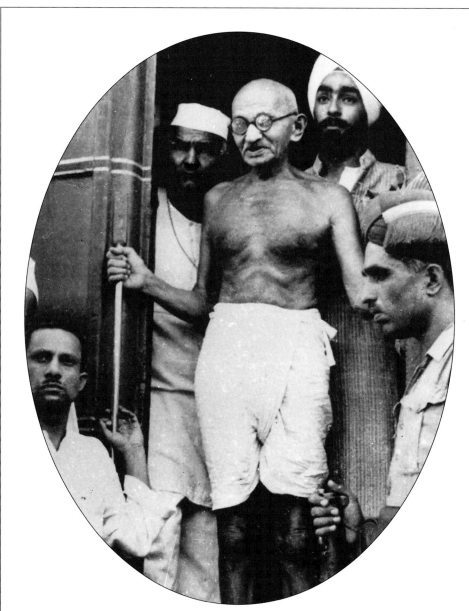

Gandhi greeting a crowd from the steps of a train, 1938.

CHAPTER SIX

FREEDOM AND DEATH

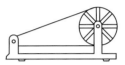

For the next decade, Gandhi devoted most of his energy to social work on behalf of the untouchables. Thinking that he had too much influence on the affairs of the Congress, he retired from it in 1934. He remained in close touch, however, through constant communication with Nehru and Patel. Frequent travel, hard work, and occasional fasts put an enormous strain on his health, both physical and mental. As he became more and more fragile, it seemed as if his career might be slowing down. In fact, the greatest struggle of his life was yet to come.

Gandhi had taken to referring to untouchables as "Harijans," or "Children of God." In 1933, he founded a new paper, *Harijan*, to deal with the issues of untouchability. It was financed by the industrialist G. D. Birla. In August, the Mahatma was released from jail and in November, he began a twelve-thousand-mile pilgrimage throughout India. It took him nine months and its purpose

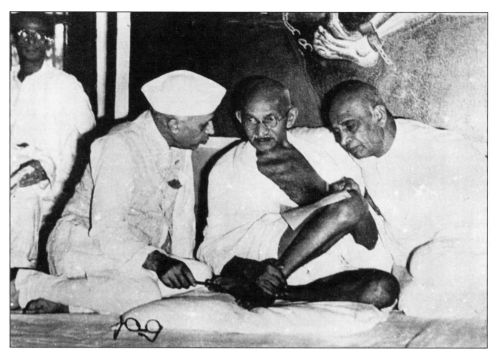

Nehru, Gandhi, and Patel in conference.

was to persuade caste Hindus to give up prejudice toward Harijans. He had to interrupt the journey in March 1934 to visit Bihar, which had suffered a serious earthquake. He announced that the earthquake was God's punishment for untouchability. Tagore disagreed, saying that orthodox Hindus could just as easily say it was a sign from God that Gandhi's campaign must be abandoned. Gandhi persisted in his view but said that orthodox Hindus were free to make their own interpretations. These interpretations led them to harass the pilgrimage for Harijans with jeering crowds and black flags. The journey continued steadily on foot from village to village while Mirabehn supervised Bapu's traveling household.

They finished the trip in June and Gandhi was on his way to attend a welcoming speech at Pune when a bomb was thrown at the lead car of his entourage. Fortunately, he and Kasturba were riding in the second car, but seven people were injured. The Mahatma was undisturbed about his own safety, saying that if he were martyred, "it will help my work for the Harijans."

Gandhi was now based at Sevagram. This was a new ashram at Wardha, a remote place in central India. In January 1936, an American woman named Margaret Sanger came to visit. She was an authority on birth control and sex education. In the course of their discussions it became clear that Gandhi and Sanger would never ever agree on the issues. The vow of brahmacharya, or

Mud hut at Sevagram Ashram, Wardha.

chastity, which Gandhi had taken in 1906 was based on ancient Hindu tradition. It meant that he viewed sex solely as a means of creating children. Sex for pleasure, even between man and wife, was a sin. He saw sex to make children as love, and sex for pleasure as lust. Therefore, any form of birth control other than abstinence was sinful because it encouraged lust. Furthermore, Gandhi thought that lust was only a man's sin. He did not believe that women enjoyed sex and therefore men's lust was a terrible insult to women's bodies. Margaret Sanger was stunned by Gandhi's arguments against contraceptives. Nevertheless, when she left Wardha she continued her lecture tour and discovered that not many Indians were so strongly opposed to artificial birth control as Gandhi. She was greeted warmly by Rabindranath Tagore and later by the sister of Jawaharlal Nehru.

Margaret Sanger.

Meanwhile, the Mahatma remained in the isolation of Wardha. He began another ashram, wrote for *Harijan*, and refined the concept of satyagraha. He watched with concern the political developments in Europe, which seemed headed for worldwide violence. Adolph Hitler, founder of the National Socialist Workers' Party, or Nazi Party, had bullied his way into the leadership of Germany and was proceeding to take over the rest of Europe. Gandhi did not especially mind that Britain was threatened. What did upset him were Hitler's brutal and warlike attitudes. In 1939, World War II began. By 1940, France had fallen and England fought alone. Many people thought she was doomed to come under Hitler's tyranny. In 1941, Japan attacked the United States and the war became truly worldwide. Gandhi wrote an open letter to Hitler explaining the futility of war. "It is a marvel to me that you do not see that it is nobody's monopoly. If not the British, then some other power will certainly improve upon your method and beat you with your own weapon. . . . I therefore appeal to you in the name of humanity to stop the war."

Gandhi did not understand that Hitler was a truly evil man who would not and could not grasp the philosophy of nonviolence. Nor did he consider that the Japanese, who were using Hitler's methods to conquer Asian countries, would probably be much harsher masters of India than the British. But the turmoil throughout the world drove Gandhi into deep despair. He became extremely irritable and the ashram suffered as a result. His secretary, Mahadev Desai, kept up a constant diplomatic struggle to reason with Gandhi and to soothe the frazzled nerves of the community.

When World War II began, England included India in the declaration of war without asking what the Indians thought. Resentment was strong and in the Congress, resistance to aiding Britain's war effort formed. Some wanted to take advantage of England's desperate situation to press for immediate independence. Only a free India, they said, would be willing to fight against the forces of tyranny. Gandhi, however, was opposed to war under any conditions. He said that to take advantage of Britain's weakness was not the way of nonviolence. He launched a campaign of individual resistance. First he asked Vinobha Bhave, one of his most important disciples, to make antiwar speeches. When Bhave was arrested, Gandhi asked Nehru to be next. Then it was Vallabhbhai Patel's turn. The program went on for nearly a year while the Japanese moved ever closer. They occupied Thailand, then Malaya, Hong Kong, Singapore, Java, Sumatra, and, finally, Rangoon, the capital of Burma, next door to India.

On March 22, 1942, Sir Stafford Cripps, a member of British Prime Minister Winston Churchill's War Cabinet, arrived in New Delhi to confer with Indian leaders about India's role in the war. He was a remarkable choice for the job, as he was a friend of Nehru and very interested in freedom for India, while Churchill himself was strongly opposed to it. Churchill's main purpose in sending the Cripps mission was to impress U.S. President Roosevelt, who had questioned Britain's rule of India. Sir Stafford offered the Indians Dominion status in return for complete cooperation with the British against the Japanese. After the war they would have the right to secede from the British Commonwealth at any time. There was a difficulty in that any state in India could secede separately and become an independent nation. Many states were run by local

Sir Stafford Cripps speaking to Gandhi, 1942.

princes. Others had a majority of Muslims. It would be possible for India to break up into several hundred small countries. Gandhi was outraged when Cripps showed him the proposal. He also saw any sort of participation in a war effort as a violation of the doctrine of nonviolence. "If this is your entire proposal to India," Gandhi said to Cripps, "I would advise you to take the next plane home."

Gandhi returned to the isolation of Sevagram Ashram, but Sir Stafford did not go home immediately. He presented the proposal to the Congress. The Indian leaders might have been willing to participate in the defense of India, but, like Gandhi, they were opposed to the idea of giving India the option of disintegrating into many small countries. The Congress rejected the proposal. The Muslim

League also rejected it. So did several other groups, and when Cripps finally went home his mission had become a failure.

The Mahatma said he did not hate the English. He could not hate any people because he believed "all men are brothers." But his opposition to the British rule of India was adamant. After the Cripps mission, he sent a resolution called "Quit India" to the Congress in which he called for Britain's immediate withdrawal from India. Following some debate over details, the Congress accepted the resolution and Gandhi started a campaign to force the British out. "Leave India to God or anarchy," he said. He was sure that if the British would just leave, India could eventually sort out her problems even if there had to be temporary chaos. As a man of peace, the Mahatma could not imagine the wholesale violence and bloodshed that would accompany anarchy.

During the first few days of August 1942, Gandhi was in Bombay preaching a doctrine that sounded very close to open rebellion. "Do or die," he said. "We shall either free India or die in the attempt." Mirabehn was sent to speak to the viceroy, John Adrian Louis Hope, Lord Linlithgow. He refused to see her, so she had to leave a message with the viceroy's secretary warning of Gandhi's determination: "No crushing force will silence him. The more you crush, the more his power will spread. You are faced with two alternatives; one to declare India's independence, and the other to kill Gandhiji, and once you kill him you kill forever all hope of friendship between India and England."

Mirabehn's message was extremely serious but the British government seemed determined to ignore it. In the early morning of August 9, Gandhi, Mirabehn, Mrs. Naidu, and Mahadev Desai were arrested. Jawaharlal Nehru and dozens of members of Congress were also arrested. The next day Kasturba was arrested when she announced that she would give a speech that Gandhi himself was to have delivered at a meeting in Bombay. Violence spread across India. Police stations were burned, telegraph lines cut, railroad tracks torn up, and British officials murdered.

Gandhi had usually enjoyed life in prison because it gave him ample time to read and write. This time was different. The group was locked in the vast elegance of the Aga Khan's palace at Pune. The grounds were surrounded by a high barbed wire fence and no newspapers were permitted inside. A terrible blow came six days after the arrest when Mahadev Desai died suddenly of a heart attack. He had been Gandhi's secretary for twenty-four years.

The Aga Khan Palace, where Gandhi and followers were imprisoned in 1944.

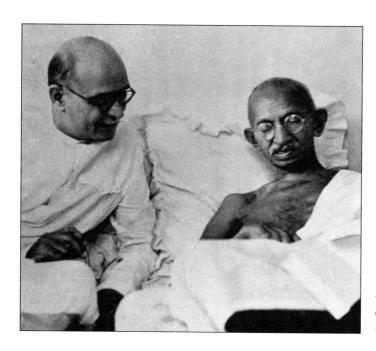

Mahadev Desai conferring with Gandhi.

"Bapu has lost his right and his left hand!" exclaimed Kasturba.

After the death, Kasturba, who had been quite fond of Desai, became depressed. At the ashrams she had had many children around her. She had enjoyed looking after them and other needy people. Locked in the palace, she could not do this kind of work. She was able to arrange for Gandhi's grandniece Manubehn Gandhi to keep her company, but this was not enough. As a diversion, Gandhi tried to teach her to read and write. He also attempted to teach her Indian geography, but she became hopelesly confused. At the age of seventy-four she could hardly be expected to develop mental skills she had never had before. She became weaker and weaker throughout the next year and had several bouts with pneumonia and bronchitis. Gandhi nursed her and treated her with natural medicines. But he refused to let her have penicillin when he learned that it would have to be injected by hypodermic needle. On the evening of February 22, 1944, Gandhi was about to take his evening walk in the palace grounds when he heard Kasturba cry out, "Bapu!" He hurried to her side. "I am going now," she said. "No one should cry after I have gone. I am at peace." A few minutes later, she died in Gandhi's arms.

The cremation, traditional in India, was accompanied by an elaborate Hindu ceremony. Afterward, Gandhi returned to

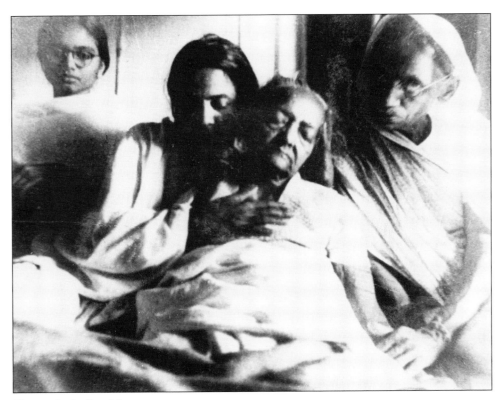

Kasturba's final hour.

Kasturba's bed. "I cannot imagine life without Ba," he said. "We lived together for sixty-two years." Bapu became so depressed he could no longer write. Six weeks after Ba's death he came down with malaria, which brought on a high fever and anemia. His doctors became seriously concerned about his health and on May 6, the Mahatma and his group were released from prison.

Within a few months, Gandhi became healthy again and returned to working toward Indian independence. In the course of his correspondence with the new viceroy, Archibald Percival Wavell, Lord Wavell, it became clear that there would be no independence before the war was over. Furthermore, independence would not be granted until Hindus and Muslims developed an agreement about how the new government would be run. Gandhi was deeply frustrated by the fact that Mohammed Ali Jinnah, leader of the Muslim League, had no intention of making such an agreement. His dream was to establish an independent Muslim state called Pakistan that would be free of any Hindu influence. Jinnah, a very arrogant man, intended to rule this state.

In the autumn of 1944, Gandhi requested a series of meetings with Jinnah in order to develop Hindu–Muslim unity. Although Jinnah was elegant, wealthy, and aloof, he and Gandhi were not exact opposites. Both men had studied law in London and were products of the British Empire. Now, both wanted the British to get out and let India solve her own problems. Jinnah had once been a member of the Congress and a strong advocate of Hindu–Muslim unity, but he had come to fear that in an independent India, the overwhelming Hindu majority would always dominate the Muslim minority. This issue made cooperation between Gandhi and Jinnah

Mohammed Ali Jinnah and Gandhi during their talks, 1944.

impossible. The American journalist Louis Fischer summed up the problem in his biography of Gandhi. Fischer wrote that India was similar to Europe in the Middle Ages because it was made up of many undeveloped small states. "Gandhi wanted to use the cement of nationalism to make it one; Jinnah wanted to use the dynamite of religion to make it two."

The talks went nowhere. Gloom and despair began to spread throughout India. Muslims, Hindus, and British were all settled into rigid positions that seemed to guarantee violence and bloodshed would have to accompany independence. There were already riots in several major cities. Clement Attlee, the new prime minister of England, who had replaced Churchill, sent a Cabinet delegation to India to seek a solution to the problem. They arrived in India on March 24, 1946. Immediately, they set up conferences and held interviews with members of the Congress and the Muslim League. But even as the terms of independence were being dis-

The Mahatma crossing a swamp in Noakhali, 1947.

cussed, India was beginning to bleed. In August, there was a three-day riot in Calcutta. In October, the Hindus in the villages of Noakhali in eastern India were brutalized by a tidal wave of murder, rape, and fire. Gandhi started a long pilgrimage through the area to persuade Hindu and Muslim leaders to set a nonviolent example for the villagers. His journey continued through January and February of 1947. Then the Hindus of the neighboring state of Bihar began to slaughter Muslims, and Gandhi was persuaded to try a peace pilgrimage there. He was accompanied by Khan Abdul Ghaffar Khan, "the Frontier Gandhi." Ghaffar Khan was a Muslim who, like Gandhi, saw no reason why Hindus and Muslims could not live together in peace.

Gandhi and Ghaffar Khan visiting Bihar, 1947.

*Gandhi calming
people in Bihar,
1947.*

On March 22, 1947, a new viceroy arrived in Delhi. He was Louis Francis Albert Victor Nicholas Mountbatten, Viscount of Burma, a naval officer related to the royal family who had been Supreme Commander of the Allied Forces in Southeast Asia during the war. Lord Mountbatten's mission, assigned to him by Prime Minister Attlee, was to arrange for India to be independent within the year by a date to be decided in negotiations. Over the years the British had consolidated several hundred independent states and principalities in India under one governmental umbrella. This remarkable feat had been achieved by building a broad system of communication, transportation, and education. The system itself had gradually strengthened a desire in the hearts of Indians to run things for themselves. As this desire grew it weakened Britain's rule. Now the administration of India had to be turned over to the people of India.

Mountbatten was to be the last viceroy, and his almost impossible task was to complete his mission in a few months. He had many separate meetings with Patel, Nehru, Jinnah, and Gandhi as well as the Chamber of Indian Princes, a group of one hundred and forty-nine maharajahs representing the various rulers of the five hundred and sixty-five princely states of India. Finally, a plan for partition into the nations of India and Pakistan on August 15, 1947, was placed before the Congress. Congress, under the leadership of Nehru, agreed. With a deep sense of despair, the Mahatma resigned himself to watching his lifelong dream melt away. Massacres began in the Punjab, and once more Bihar and Noakhali

Gandhi meeting with Mountbatten.

were swept up in rioting. Satyagraha and *ahimsa*, or nonviolence, had become meaningless.

As August approached, Gandhi decided to go to Noakhali to attempt to keep the peace when the expected violence broke out. On the way, he had to pass through Calcutta, where rioting had almost become a way of life. Mountbatten and the local authorities were afraid that Independence Day would bring outright civil war. They persuaded the Mahatma to stay a few more days before going on to Noakhali. They thought his presence would be a calming influence. Many people were surprised when Shaheed Suhrawardy,

Montbatten with count-down sign behind him.

a powerful Muslim politician who was suspected of having organized the murders and violence of the year before, asked Gandhi to
stay through August 15, Independence Day. Gandhi agreed on the
condition that Suhrawardy stay with him in the same house and
that they be seen together wherever they went in Calcutta.

*Independence
Day at the
Red Fort in
Delhi, 1947.*

The city was in tumult, but with the help of Suhrawardy, Gandhi managed to keep a shaky sort of peace. On the eve of Independence Day he spoke at a prayer meeting. He could not, however, take much pleasure in the celebration because it was also Partition Day. He pleaded for people to refrain from violence. "If communal strife spreads all over India," he said, "what use is our freedom?" On the day itself, the people of Calcutta went crazy. Everywhere Gandhi went the crowds cheered him and showered him with rose petals, but he found no joy in the celebration.

Violence rattled around India like a series of tornadoes. Some of the worst of it took place in the Punjab, a state that had been cut in two by the partition. Hindus were fleeing Pakistan and Muslims were fleeing India. There were at least fifteen million refugees and they were butchering one another on the road. On September 7, Gandhi left Calcutta for the Punjab. On the way, his train stopped in Delhi where he learned that the rioting, destruction, and killings were worse than anything seen in Calcutta. The Punjab would have to wait. For the next few months, while staying at the house of G. D. Birla, Gandhi worked with the Emergency Committee formed by Mountbatten and the Nehru government. When he visited Muslim refugee camps he sometimes heard the chant, "Death to Gandhi!" Many Hindus resented his sympathy for Muslims and also cried out "Death to Gandhi!" Efforts for peace seemed almost hopeless and there was talk of war between India and Pakistan. Claiming responsibility for the fierce hostility and the horrible devastation it produced, the frail Mahatma began a fast on January 13, 1948. He ended it five days later when a resolution to maintain peace was signed by more than one hundred and thirty representa-

ABOVE:
*Partition
refugees on
the road.*

LEFT:
*A trainload
of partition
refugees.*

His "walking sticks," as Gandhi called Manubehn and Abhabehn, help Bapu walk to an evening prayer meeting in the garden at Birla House, 1948.

tives of Muslim and Hindu groups. They feared that Gandhi's death would have brought on civil war.

On January 30, still weak from the fast, Gandhi went to lead his daily prayer meeting in the garden of Birla House. Manubehn and another grandniece, Abhabehn, were supporting him as he walked when a man pushed out of the crowd, bowed in front of the Mahatma, and shot him three times. Gandhi fell, calling, "Hai, Rama." *Rama* is the Hindu name for God, and every good Hindu hopes to die with that name on his lips. Manubehn and Abhabehn cradled Bapu's head as he died, blood spreading across his white khadi clothing. The assassin was caught almost immediately after an intense struggle. At the police station it was found that his name was Nathuram Godse and that he was a Hindu extremist who was a member of a group that was angry with Gandhi for what they saw as his betrayal of ancient Hindu tradition.

Later that evening, Prime Minister Jawaharlal Nehru went on All-India Radio. "The light has gone out of our lives and there is

In the garden at Birla House, stone footsteps show Gandhi's path to the spot where he was assassinated.

Gandhi was cremated according to Hindu custom.

darkness everywhere. . . . Our beloved leader, Bapu as we called him, the father of our nation, is no more." Nehru was speaking extemporaneously. His voice was shaky and hoarse. "The light has gone out, I said, and yet I was wrong. . . . The light that has illumined this country for these many years will illumine this country for many more years, and a thousand years later that light will still be seen in this country and the world will see it."

Gandhiji's old friend and colleague Tagore had noticed that light many years before. He said of the Mahatma, "He will always be remembered as one who made his life a lesson for all ages to come."

◆ *The cities and towns named on the above map are places important to Gandhi's career in India. The darker shaded areas were part of British India but became the independent Muslim country of Pakistan on the day of Indian Independence, August 15, 1947. (East Pakistan became a separate republic called Bangladesh in December 1971.) State names and fine lines denote states that make up India today.*

GUIDE TO PRONUNCIATION

Ahmedabad	AHM-deh-bahd
Bhagavad Gita	BAH-gah-vahd GHEE-tah
Bhave (Vinobha)	BHAH-veh
Charkha	CHAR-kah
Delhi	DEL-ee
Gandhi	GAHN-dee
Gokhale	GO-kah-leh
Gujarat	GOO-jah-raht
Jawaharlal (Nehru)	Jah-wah-HAR-lal
Khadi	KAH-dee
Mahatma	Mah-HAHT-mah
Mohandas	Mo-HAHN-das
Pune	POO-neh
Rajkot	RAHJ-kote
Satyagraha	SAHT-yah-grah-hah
Swaraj	Swah-RAHJ

ALEXANDER, HORACE. *Gandhi Through Western Eyes.* Philadelphia: New Society Publishers, 1984.

ANDREWS, C. F. *Mahatma Gandhi's Ideas.* New York: Macmillan, 1930.

ATTENBOROUGH, RICHARD. *In Search of Gandhi.* London: The Bodley Head, 1982.

BANERJEE, HIRANMAY. *Rabindranath Tagore.* New Delhi: Publications Division, Ministry of Information and Broadcasting, 1989.

BROWN, JUDITH M. *Gandhi, Prisoner of Hope.* New Haven: Yale University Press, 1991.

COLLINS, LARRY AND DOMINIQUE LAPIERRE. *Freedom at Midnight.* New York: Simon and Schuster, 1975.

DESAI, NARAYAN, TR. BHAL MALJI. *Bliss Was It To Be Young—With Gandhi, Childhood Reminiscences.* Bombay: Bharatiya Vidya Bhavan, 1988.

ERIKSON, ERIK H. *Gandhi's Truth: On the Origins of Militant Non-violence.* New York: W. W. Norton & Company, Inc., 1969.

FISCHER, LOUIS. *The Life of Mahatma Gandhi.* New York: Harper & Brothers, 1950.

GANDHI, MAHATMA. *Young India.* New York: B. W. Huebsch Inc., 1924.

GANDHI, MOHANDAS K. *All Men Are Brothers.* New York: Continuum, 1994.

———. *An Autobiography: The Story of My Experiments with Truth.* Boston: Beacon Press, 1957.

———. *Gandhi on Non-violence: Selected Texts.* New York: New Directions, 1965.

GANDHI, RAJMOHAN. *The Good Boatman, A Portrait of Gandhi.* New Delhi: Viking Penguin India, 1995.

MANDELA, NELSON. *Long Walk to Freedom.* Boston: Little, Brown, 1994.

MEHTA, VED. *Mahatma Gandhi and His Apostles.* New York: Viking Press, 1976.

NAIPAUL, V. S. *India: A Wounded Civilization.* New York: Knopf, 1977.

NEHRU, JAWAHARLAL. *Jawaharlal Nehru, An Autobiography.* Delhi: Oxford University Press, 1985.

———. *Nehru on Gandhi, A Selection from Writings and Speeches of Jawaharlal Nehru.* New York: John Day, 1948.

OATES, STEPHEN B. *Let the Trumpet Sound, The Life of Martin Luther King, Jr.* New York: Harper & Row, 1982.

PAYNE, ROBERT. *The Life and Death of Mahatma Gandhi.* New York: Dutton, 1960.

SHAHANI, RANJEE. *Mr. Gandhi.* New York: Macmillan, 1961.

SHIRER, WILLIAM L. *Gandhi, A Memoir.* New York: Simon & Schuster, 1979.

SHRIDHARANI, KRISHNALAL. *The Mahatma and the World.* New York: Duell, Sloan and Pearce, 1946.

UPADHYAYA, J. M. *Mahatma Gandhi As a Student.* New Delhi: Publication Division, Ministry of Information and Broadcasting, Government of India, 1994.

WOLPERT, STANLEY. *India.* Berkeley: University of California Press, 1991.

ACKNOWLEDGMENTS

AND PICTURE CREDITS

The Mahatma would have asserted that he was not different from the rest of humanity, that we are all brothers and sisters together. I am glad he was human like all of us, but I am thankful he was also different like all of us. Humanity is the sum of our individuality.

The individuals at Clarion Books, especially Dorothy Briley, have been wonderfully supportive of this project. For help in obtaining photographs, I thank Dr. N. Radhakrishnan, Director of the Gandhi Smriti and Darshan Samiti at Birla House in New Delhi and the staff of its photography department. Also, I owe a substantial debt of gratitude to the people at the National Gandhi Museum, Rajghat, New Delhi; R. G. Turakhia, Anand Shewawe, Ram Sanyan Sharma, and particularly to J. B. Chadha.

Kirit D. Shukla, who was our driver, guide, and mentor for six days in Gujarat, deserves special recognition for making sure that my wife Sylvia and I savored the full flavor of Gandhi's home state. And

Sylvia herself must be thanked for being a valiant traveler. After visiting two Gandhi museums in Delhi, the Sabarmati Ashram Museum in Ahmedabad, Gandhi's childhood haunts in Rajkot, and his birthplace in Porbandar, she could have acted as a competent docent when we finally reached Mani Bhavan Museum in Bombay.

JOHN B. SEVERANCE

PICTURE CREDITS

Italics refer to photos

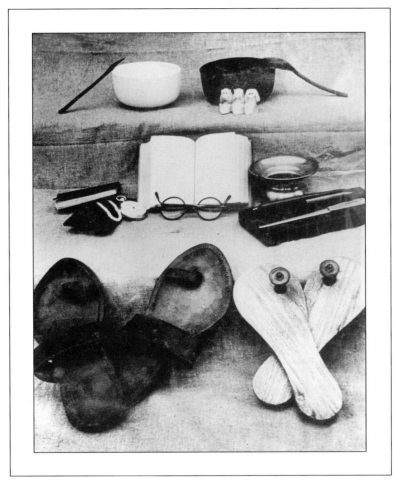

Gandhi's possessions at the time of his death.